Reason To Believe

Maurice Wiles

Trinity Press International
Harrisburg, Pennsylvania

First North American Edition 1999
by Trinity Press International,
P.O. Box 1321, Harrisburg, PA 17105
Trinity Press International is a division of the Morehouse Group.

Cover art: *Accent en rose* by Wassily Kandinsky, Copyright 2000 Artists Rights Society (ARS), NY/ADAGP, Musee National d'Art Moderne, Centre Georges Pompidou, Paris, France. Giraudon/Art Resource, NY.
Cover design: Jim Booth

Note: A study guide for this book is available at www.trinitypressintl.com

Library of Congress Cataloging-in-Publication Data

Wiles, Maurice F.
    Reason to believe/Maurice Wiles.
        p. cm.
    Includes bibliographical references and index.
    ISBN 1-56338-305-5 (pbk.: alk. paper)
    1. Theology, Doctrinal—Popular works. 1. Title.

BT77. W49 2000
230—dc21

99-047656

Typeset by Rowland Phototypesetting Ltd
Bury St Edmunds, England
and printed in the United States of America

For Paddy and Ellen

Contents

Preface

In this book I propose to set out as simply and as clearly as I can what seem to me appropriate responses to some of the most basic questions about Christian belief that perplex many people both inside and outside the church. It is no easy undertaking, primarily because the issues themselves are anything but simple. My own work as a theologian over a good many years has certainly reinforced my awareness of the complexity of the issues involved and the difficulty of determining how best to deal with the problems that they raise. But those years have not undermined my conviction that, despite all the difficulties inherent in Christian belief, Christianity does point us, however indirectly, to a true way of understanding the world and of living in it.

So the task is one that ought not to be shirked. Christianity is a faith that claims to be open to all, and it would be odd to claim that serious consideration of the basic issues of Christian faith is not something that thinking people can be expected to engage in and that any insights into them that scholarly reflection may be able to provide are incapable of wider dissemination. Twin dangers lie in wait on the path that needs to be followed: on the one hand the danger of oversimplifying the issues in a way that distorts the truth, and on the other that of allowing their real complexities to lure me back into using the technical language that is the private preserve of the specialist scholar. I have tried to avoid them both. Whether I have succeeded I must leave to the reader to decide. At least I set out in full awareness of the difficulties.

It is not my expectation that the account I give will convince the sceptic and lead him or her to embrace Christian faith. Such changes do happen; but they are not often the direct result of reasoned discussion or argument. They are more often set in train by some life-changing experience, like a bereavement or the birth of a child, or arise out of the impact made by the life of a Christian friend or congregation. But that is not to discount the importance of reasoned reflection on these difficult issues. For most Christians, however they may have come to embark on the road of Christian discipleship, there are times when the difficulties inherent in Christian belief seem to make it almost impossible to accept. Such moments should not simply be dismissed, as if they were symptoms of a reprehensible lack of faith. The difficulties are real and we need to acknowledge them. I do not believe that this book solves them – to believe that would indeed be to have succumbed to the way of oversimplification. But it is my hope that it may help some people to think them through in ways that will lead them to see Christian belief as something that can reasonably be affirmed without having simply to shut our eyes to difficulties of which we cannot help but be aware.

It is tempting to begin a book of this kind with an introductory section, explaining the assumptions and principles on which its account of Christian faith is based. I have resisted that temptation and have started straight in with the substance of Christian faith. But from time to time, especially in the earlier part of the book, I have interposed at appropriate places short sections that do not deal so directly with substantive matters of Christian belief, but rather with some of the underlying issues that need to be taken into account in determining how we can reasonably assess the claims of Christianity. Some are concerned with cultural or philosophical matters, such as the use of language or symbolism, which are crucial to reasoned reflection on the formulation of beliefs about God; others discuss more factual and historical questions, such as the nature of the biblical documents and the modern study of them. These sections are printed in bold type, but I have tried to pitch them at the same level as the main discussion of the faith itself, not assuming any greater measure of prior knowledge or making use of any more technical terms.

I have avoided using footnotes or references which have a tendency to break up the flow of the argument. But there is a list of books at the end for those who want to follow up in more detail any of the lines of argument that are set out here only in very brief, outline form. The precise references of citations and allusions to the Bible that occur from time to time in the text are also listed in an index at the back of the book.

The book would never have been written without the support of family and friends. First and foremost I am indebted to my wife, Paddy, for the original suggestion that I write such a book, for her sustained refusal to accept my many excuses for not doing so and for her careful reading of earlier versions of the text. John Bowden's interest and encouragement from the start was also influential in getting the project off the ground. I am grateful to him for that, as for his friendship and help as publisher over many years. Special thanks are also due to Arnold Bradshaw, Lucy and Peter Collings, Leslie Houlden, Belinda Jack, Pemma Spencer-Chapman, Peter Walker and Ellen Wiles, who all generously undertook to read through an earlier draft of the book, which has greatly benefited from their comments and suggestions. Its shortcomings are my responsibility, not theirs, but they are at least less than they would otherwise have been. Further thanks are due to my granddaughter Ellen, who thought up the idea for the cover and took the photograph for it.

I

Beginnings

God or the Big Bang?

'In the beginning, God . . .'. That is how the Bible begins. It is also, according to Christian belief, how everything began. It seems therefore an appropriate place for this book to begin. But can we begin there? Or is that to jump over one of the biggest problems of all? Through all the centuries over which the Bible was written, belief in God or the gods was a more or less universal assumption. People might vary a great deal in what they believed about God. But belief in God or the gods as such was a fundamental aspect of how people made sense of the world around them and ordered their lives in it. Today's culture could hardly be more different. For many, belief in God is an irrelevance, if not a positive hindrance, to their understanding of the world and their way of living in it. Even for many Christians, fundamental as belief in God may be, it is a deeply puzzling notion. What do we mean by the word? What kind of belief in God is compatible with the beliefs about the world that Christians share with their surrounding culture?

The dominant feature of that surrounding culture is the advance of scientific knowledge, which has vastly increased our understanding of the world and of human persons. Its influence on how we see things is all-pervasive. But there are aspects of our experience that continue to resist incorporation into its comprehensive vision. For example, in spite of all the remarkable and rapidly increasing insights into the working of the human brain, consciousness remains a puzzling phenomenon that seems to have no well-defined place in this expanding network of new knowledge. Yet it would be absurd to dismiss it as irrelevant or unreal. So there are important realities that cannot be convincingly fitted into the dominant scientific mode of interpreting the world. Perhaps God, like consciousness, is another reality of which the same is true. Of course the analogy is not exact. God does not impinge on our experience with the same undeniable immediacy as human consciousness. But the analogy at least serves to remind us that the notion of God, which has been so central to human history and human culture, cannot be set on one side simply on the ground that our scientific culture finds no place for it. Whether the notion is one that can rightly command our assent is, of course, a further question and not one that can be settled as easily as that. But at least the idea that it can be ruled out of court from the outset is without justification, and we can properly begin where we proposed to begin.

'In the beginning, God created the heaven and the earth. And the earth was without form, and void.' The words get the Book of Genesis off to a firm and confident start. But the question we have to put is this: are they words that we can take over and make our own? And if we can, will we be able to speak them in the same firm and confident tone? One thing we can be pretty sure of. If we are able to make them our own, we will not be understanding them in precisely the same way that the author of the Book of Genesis did. He, like most of his contemporaries in the ancient world, thought of creation as giving shape to formless matter. The world was without form, and God's creative work was to give it form. And in the Greek world in which Christianity first grew up and developed its beliefs, the understanding of creation was of a similar kind. Yet Christians soon came to embrace a more radical understanding of creation. The majesty of the God in whom they had come to believe was not adequately reflected in a God whose role was simply to give form to formless matter that had somehow always existed alongside God. God was supreme, and creation must be understood to involve also the bringing into being of matter itself. This stronger sense of creation, 'creation out of nothing' as it has usually been called, has remained a distinctive feature of Christian belief ever since. And that fundamental feature of what Christians mean by creation is crucial to the way in which we relate Christian belief to modern scientific accounts. Christians are not setting out to provide their own account of the way the physical world began; they are not offering an alternative account in opposition to the theory of the big bang. The big bang is the furthest point to which we can trace back the causal story of the stages through which our physical universe has developed into its present state. The question which the idea of the world as created by God is concerned with is a distinct, though related one; it is the question how it is that there is anything at all. But even if that rescues the notion of God as creator from the common objection that it is in conflict with well-established truths of modern science, that's not enough in itself to justify us in affirming it. For it is certainly a strange claim to make. What grounds have we for making it? Do we even know what we mean by it?

Basic to such a claim is an underlying conviction that the physicists' account, however true in itself, does not constitute a full and complete explanation. A fundamental root to both science and religion is a sense of wonder. It is that sense of wonder that fuels all human endeavour to understand our-selves and our world. The progress of scientific knowledge has provided answers to many aspects of that innate sense of wonder. The work of evolutionary biologists and of cosmolo-gists has revealed for us the processes by which we and our world developed from their primeval origins to the com-plexity of life as we now know it. And future scientific dis-coveries will no doubt continue to shed further light on those processes. So it is not surprising that to persevere with talk of God's role in creation should seem to many to be a strange and inappropriate thing to do. Its strangeness is not to be denied; it is not easy to be clear just what such a claim might mean. But before we abandon it, we need to stop and reflect how strange is the alternative available to us. The scientific account tells us of a primeval explosion of gases in the far distant past, from which by a process of physical, chemical and biological changes has emerged the world that we inhabit. But that world is not simply a world of physical objects blindly interacting with one another; it is a world which includes self-consciousness, the ability of one part of the world to formulate and pursue questions about its own origins and nature; it is a world characterized by the experience of beauty and by the drawing of distinctions between good and evil. However we classify such fundamental features of our human existence, they are of a different order from those purely physical forces that were so powerfully at work in the earliest moments of the history of the universe. Can we really be content to say that the scientific account of the beginnings of the universe and of its evolutionary development (or any imaginable future development of that kind of account) constitutes a full and complete explanation of the sense of wonder to which reflection on the world gives rise? Is it right to dismiss the feeling that there may be other things of a different kind that also need to be said as nothing more than a delusion? The basic instinct of wonder from which both science and religion spring ought not to be so easily satisfied. It is the refusal of this fundamental sense of wonder to be silenced, despite the ceaseless clatter of technological achievement, that prompts many people, including many scientists, to persist in saying 'In the beginning God'. And when they say that, they are not envisaging God as a separate cause, responsible for inserting the non-physical aspects of our world, such as consciousness, beauty and morality, into a physical structure that can be fully explained in other ways. That would be to revert to the older idea of a God who gives form to formless matter, which Christianity abandoned as inadequate very early in its history. In any case consciousness is far too intimately linked to its physical basis for such a radical separation to be acceptable. It is rather a matter of whether our thirst for explanation of a world endowed with such properties as consciousness, beauty and morality can ever be satisfied with an account that sees them simply as the by-product of a chance collocation of atoms and allows no place to them, or anything like them, in its account of the origination of the world.

Underlying the affirmation of God as creator, then, is the conviction that if we are to be true to the human search for understanding, there are other kinds of enquiry, in addition to the researches of the scientist, that need to be pursued. But can that conviction be more than a protest against the acceptance of the way of the scientist as the only responsible way of furthering our knowledge and understanding of the world? When we say 'In the beginning God', what content can we give to the word 'God'? Might we as well say: 'In the beginning X'? The route of reflection that I am following may not enable us to say very much; but there are some things it does enable us to say.

The 'God' to whom these reflections point us cannot be a physical entity, or God would be picked up somewhere in the web of the scientists' researches. God must, that is to say, be incorporeal. The point can be put in a more general way. If God is the source of all existence, that which makes it possible for anything at all to exist, God cannot be just one more thing within the universe, however much greater or more powerful than everything else. God must be a reality of a higher order than we experience directly within the world. God must be, to use a rather technical term, 'transcendent' in relation to us and to our world.

Furthermore, since it was things like the ordered nature of the world and the human capacity to discover that order, delight in beauty and the pursuit of the good, that prompted our dissatisfaction with the idea of the scientific account as the only proper style of explanation of the world, it seems reasonable to envisage the nature of God as bearing a positive relation to these things. The world is, of course, characterized by ugliness and evil as well as by beauty and goodness. That is a major difficulty for any form of Christian belief; indeed it is almost certainly the greatest difficulty about belief for most readers – as it is for me. I am not going to deal with that intractable problem now; we shall come back to consider it at length at a later stage, when we will be in a position to do so in relation to an understanding of Christian faith that has already gone through a process of critical reflection. But for the moment it seems fair to say that in our ordinary understanding of the world, we tend to ascribe a more positive role to the virtues than to the vices. We look for intelligibility in the world, and the order that we find seems not to be something that we simply choose to impose on it but something that belongs to the structure of things. In the search for beauty and the pursuit of goodness, we do not regard ourselves as acting in a purely arbitrary manner; despite all the variety of aesthetic and moral judgments, the wrongness of cruelty to children, for example, is rooted in the way the world is constituted and not just the free decision of any human society. And this gives us ground for seeing order, beauty and goodness as pointers towards the nature of God. Furthermore neither the enjoyment of beauty nor the unselfish virtues, such as compassion, seem to receive any fully convincing explanation in the evolutionary story that science tells. But they are the sources of some of life's deepest joys now, and the latter, at least, have also a crucial role to play in ensuring the survival of human life on this planet into the future. Explanations of our world that fail to give some adequate account of them fall short not only at the level of theory but also in terms of what is of vital practical importance.

So the sense of wonder does not fuel only scientific enquiry. In the past it has fuelled other forms of enquiry, including the religious. And there are good reasons why it should continue to do so. Starting from scratch, which is what we have been seeking to do up to now, may not take us very far – though I have argued that the idea of God to which it points is not entirely vacuous, not just a pure unknown. But we never do start from scratch, in religion or in science. In both cases we inevitably start with the accumulated wisdom of the past, which provides the indispensable launching pad for new insights and discoveries, while itself always needing to be revised in the light of the new things it enables us to learn. So, for the Christian, the concept of God comes already fleshed out as the God to whom the Bible bears witness, the God and Father of Jesus Christ. Indeed, whether we are believers or not, developed ideas of God are part of the culture that surrounds us, and affect in one direction or another the way we react to any contemporary talk about God.

This means that there is another way in which Christians may choose to approach the task of answering the question: what do we understand by the words 'In the beginning God'? We can choose to start our reflections not with the general and broadly accepted human experience of the world or the specialized development of it that makes up modern scientific knowledge, but with what the Bible and Christian doctrine have to say about God. Indeed some Christians believe that that is the only proper starting point for reflection about God. But the kind of reflection with which I began seems to me important, however imprecise the conclusions at which it is able to arrive. It provides a contemporary context where talk about God may be seen to have a place and a purpose – and that is not at all obvious without some such preliminary reflection. One of the main disincentives to religious belief today is the difficulty to see what role it might have to play in our scientific age. That anxiety I have tried to meet. But there is a further widely-felt disincentive, namely doubt whether the specifically Christian understanding of God is one that is adequate to that context. That further anxiety I will try to meet in what follows, as we pursue the second, complementary approach of seeing how the biblical conception of God and the traditional Christian understanding that has developed in the course of the church's life fit our modern understanding of the world and of ourselves.

Interlude I: Language

Before we go any further along that road, we need to pause and look in a little more detail at one of the issues that has arisen so far. God, I have argued, is that mysterious reality on which the very existence of any world at all depends, and it is a mistake to think of God as simply one more item in the world, even incomparably the greatest item. If that is how we ought to think about God, then there is obviously a problem about how we can find appropriate words and concepts to do so. Language originally developed to help us deal with the objects and experiences we meet with in the world. So is it competent to deal with God? Can our human words, words that have grown up in such a different environment, express truth about the 'transcendent' God? Can we speak about God at all?

Obviously people do speak about God. We don't have to set about inventing a way of speaking about God from scratch. We inherit traditional ways of doing so. But those ways didn't emerge ready-made, like Athene from the head of Zeus. They developed over long periods of time, and it is helpful to understand how they arose and how they function. For like other aspects of tradition, we don't simply take them over without scrutiny. In the process of learning how to use them, we also modify them. Language is a continually evolving phenomenon, and language about God is no exception.

A familiar hymn begins with the line:

Immortal, invisible, God only wise.

That phrase makes use of the two basic strategies that are used in speaking about God. On the one hand there is a negative approach. Many of the most fundamental features of our finite, physical existence do not apply to God. To make sure that this basic truth does not get overlooked, a lot of the words we use about God are, like the first two words of the hymn, negative in form and implication: God is 'immortal', not subject to death; and God is 'invisible', not open to being apprehended by human vision. Such language has an important role in counteracting the natural tendency to think of God in ways too close to our experience of people and things around us. But by itself it does not tell us what God is like, only what God is not like.

So there is a second, positive approach, reflected in the last two words of the line from the hymn. I have already argued that it is the strange experience of beauty and goodness, and the emergence of consciousness within our finite, physical world that prompt the sense of wonder that invokes the name of God. So we take the words that we use to name such things in ordinary life, and use them as pointers towards the nature of the mysterious God. But we have to recognize that when they are used of God, they cannot have exactly the same force as when they are used of people or things in the world. The hymn makes the point by calling God '*only* wise'. God alone is truly wise; human wisdom, built up by the distillation of a narrow range of limited human experience, is at its best no more than a pale shadow of God's wisdom. We can have only the faintest glimmer of understanding of what that is really like.

There is another, perhaps more natural, way of putting this second, positive form of language about God. Human language originally developed as a way of coping with the physical world around us. That is the context of its most basic usage. So it is natural to see that context as providing its primary sense, and to regard its use to speak about the immortal, invisible God as a secondary extended sense. Many of the words we use to refer to God have a more obviously human or physical connotation than wisdom. Let us take the traditional term 'Father' as an example. The Epistle to the Ephesians does speak of God as 'the Father from whom all fatherhood in heaven and earth takes its name'. That is looking at the matter in the same way that the hymn views wisdom; it is to imply that the word 'father' is only being used in its strictest and fullest sense when it is used to refer to God. We do not have to deny that there is a sense in which that may be true, while at the same time claiming that linguistically the matter is better put the other way round. 'Father' is the word used to describe the male progenitor of another human being, and carries with it associated connotations of love, nurture and authority. But our use of the word is not restricted to its literal meaning; we do not confine our use of it to male parents. We also use it metaphorically in a wide range of contexts: Nelson Mandela is called the father of the new South Africa; or again, more abstractly, we speak of the wish as father to the thought. Not all the characteristics of a literal father are applicable in these varied metaphorical uses of the word. There needs to be enough structural similarity between the two uses, literal fatherhood and that to which the term is applied metaphorically, for the general force of what is being said to be intelligible to the hearer. But, even more importantly, a good metaphor is designed to tease the hearer's imagination into new and richer understandings of the situation the metaphor has been used to describe. (The use of the word 'tease' is, in fact, quite a good illustration of the point in question; good-natured teasing can provoke fruitful self-questioning, where more direct criticism would have failed in its goal and been met only with resentment and rejection.) When we use the word 'father' with reference to God, it is an extension of this metaphorical use. It implies a conviction that the God of whom we speak is the ultimate source of our existence and one whose own being is not wholly alien to ours; moreover that God's relation to us is one characterized by love, nurture and authority. Some of the characteristics of a literal human father, such as gender and sex, we may say, are not applicable to God at all. But they may, nonetheless, as contemporary discussion has done much to bring out, have had in the past and still continue to have a distorting effect on how we imagine and conceive of God. Just how the characteristics that *are* applicable are to be understood when applied to God is an open question. If using the word 'father' implies that God is personal, what sort of person does it imply, since God cannot be a person in the way a physical human being is? How does God exercise love, nurture and authority in relation to us?

Speaking of God as father does not convey precise information on such topics; it serves rather to stimulate the imagination to reflect creatively about them. It is an imaginative and creative use of language, but it is also a risky one. It can enlighten, but it can also mislead.

So far I have been speaking as if each of us had to be the imaginative creator of appropriate metaphors in order to be able to think or speak about God at all. But of course it is not like that. We do not have to reinvent the wheel with every new generation. Just as we inherit a well-established tradition of words and concepts with which we think and speak about moral, social or aesthetic matters, so we do in matters of religion. Today, we are aware in all those spheres of a far greater variety of traditions than people were aware of in the past; and that complicates, confuses and unsettles our ideas and our practice. But it is still the case that for most people there is a basic tradition about God which shapes the way they think and speak about religious questions from the outset; and that is so whether or not they consider there is truth to be found there. This makes it all the more important that we do not lose sight of the way language about God works. If it is really language about God and not about some human substitute for God, it must of necessity be indirect, suggestive, tentative and exploratory in character; it cannot be clear-cut, precise or definitive.

So in the ensuing reflections about some of the widely-felt difficulties in relation to many traditional beliefs about God, this is something we will need continually to bear in mind. It applies even, indeed perhaps with special force, to language that has been made familiar and endowed with an aura of sanctity by long usage in the life of the church. The difficulties that we shall be meeting are real enough, but some of them seem more acute than they should because of our false expectations about the kind of precision and certainty that is possible in the case of affirmations about God.

2

The God of the Bible

*Does God or chance determine
what happens in the world?*

In the opening chapter I spoke of belief in God or the gods as a virtually universal belief in the world out of which the biblical books emerged. I then went on to reflect on the idea of God as creator that finds expression in the Bible's opening words. But those early, basic beliefs were not primarily in God as creator; they were more a matter of God as the one who controlled the mixture of good and evil fortune, of happiness and calamity that makes up the human lot. And it is that latter concern that figures more prominently in the Bible as well. The central theme of the first five interconnected books of the Bible, known as the Pentateuch, is how God chose the people of Israel, was the directing hand behind the ups and downs of their early history, and eventually established them in their own land. The point the writer is particularly making in the first of those five books, the book of Genesis, is that, unlike the gods of the surrounding nations, the God who guides the destiny of Israel is also the God who created and controls the forces of nature. And so the account of the creation is the start of the story of Israel's history, and is told in appropriate story form. God takes the dust of the earth, fashions the figure of a man and then breathes into his nostrils the breath of life so that he becomes a living creature. We don't (or certainly don't need to) have any difficulty in treating that as a pictorial expression of our ultimate dependence on God for our existence as human beings. There are no grounds there for any conflict with the evolutionary story that science has disclosed, unless we make the perverse choice to read it as pure history.

But what of the way the story goes on? In all the history that follows, an active, determining role is ascribed to God. The ways in which God brings about the particular desired ends in the unfolding story are varied. Sometimes it is by divine inspiration of the heroes of faith: the visionary experience of the burning bush gives Moses the courage to go to Pharaoh and demand the liberation of the Israelites. Sometimes it involves miraculous happenings of doubtful credibility and questionable morality: it took the death of every firstborn child and animal throughout Egypt in a single night finally to secure that liberation. Sometimes it is evil human actions that are used by God to bring about his purposes: when jealousy led Joseph's brothers to sell him into slavery and pretend to his father that he had been killed by a wild beast, Joseph later tells them not to reproach themselves because it was God's way of getting him to Egypt, where he could rise to a position of such authority that he could save the lives of all the family from the disaster of famine. These stories too, we may say, are to be treated as stories and enjoyed as such. Like the mythological picture of God moulding the dust of the earth, they are to be seen as legends of the kind that figure in the early history of every nation. True enough, but the parallel is not exact. The heart of the problem remains untouched. In the case of the mythological account of God forming human beings out of the dust of the earth, the underlying thrust of the story – namely that human life is not an accident of chance but ultimately derives from God – is, I have argued, one that (for all the difficulties of understanding it) still offers a valid answer to a continuing question. But can we say the same of the legends of God's active role in the history of Israel and of the human world more generally? The details of the various stories are admittedly not of great significance; we can, indeed, enjoy them as contributing to the lively legends that those stories are. But the conviction that God's providential care was directing the fortunes of

Israel from the outset – the call of Abraham, the exodus from Egypt, the acquisition of the promised land – is a central theme running right through the Old Testament as a whole. Is that also something that still offers a valid answer to a continuing question?

Before trying to answer that question we must define a bit more carefully what was involved in that sense of God's providential care. It was not something that ensured prosperity for Israel whatever the nation did. Faithfulness brought reward, and unfaithfulness corrective punishment. So when Jerusalem was captured and the leading citizens taken off to exile in Babylon in the sixth century BC, prophets could account for this by describing the disaster, not as a disproof of God's care for the nation but as a judgment on its deep-seated corruption. God's care was for faithful Israel, and particularly for the downtrodden faithful. As one of the Psalms puts it: 'The Lord feeds the hungry, deals out justice to the oppressed and protects the stranger in the land.' Moreover as time went on and the fortunes of Israel became more and more tied up with those of the surrounding nations, it was increasingly recognized that God's providential care of Israel necessarily involved God's playing a decisive role in the affairs of other nations too. So when Israel's exile in Babylon was ended by the defeat of the great Babylonian Empire by the Persians under Cyrus, the outcome of that clash between those two empires was seen as God's doing, something brought about by God with the specific purpose of securing the return of the Jews to their ancient promised land. What are we, with our modern understanding of history, to make of this way of seeing God's relation to the human story, which is so prominent a feature of the biblical record?

It is the supposed conflict between religion and science that holds pride of place in the popular imagination today. So one might expect any difficulties in relating Christian faith to history to be less daunting. No historian would think of claiming to be able to give a complete explanation of what has happened in the past. Personal and social, geographical and economic, political and religious factors are all involved. The historian draws on them all, and tries to weave them together to provide an account which will extend our understanding of how and why things have happened as they have. There is always scope for shedding further light on the past. But true as all that may be, it doesn't offer as much help with our present problem as we may be inclined to hope at first. It will already be evident that the difficulties of incorporating anything like the biblical notion of God's determining role into the way in which we normally understand our past are formidable. We must begin by spelling out a little more precisely what those difficulties are.

First, any generalized claim that God acts in history to meet the needs of the downtrodden just doesn't seem to fit the facts. That is a difficulty recognized within the Old Testament itself, as the vigorous protest of Job bears witness; he angrily repudiates his comforters' insistence that his exceptional calamities must be due to some exceptional evil on his part, however hidden from the eyes of the rest of the world. The Psalmist's assertion that God feeds the hungry and protects the stranger is belied by pictures of starving children in Africa and fleeing refugees from Kosovo appearing on our television screens.

Secondly, just as we now know the universe to be incomparably older and bigger than our forebears could ever have imagined, so also both the time-scale and the geographical range of human history are of a different order of magnitude from anything the biblical writers envisaged. This makes the biblical notion of a single divine purpose to the whole human story, working itself out under God's directing hand in the chequered history of the people of Israel, not necessarily impossible but at the very least a far less plausible notion for us than it was for them.

Thirdly, it is extremely difficult to see how such a direct divine impingement on the course of human history can be understood to operate in practice. We are much more aware today of the nature and the extent of the regularities that characterize the physical world and of the interconnectedness of happenings at the human level. Some of the divine actions of which the Bible speaks cut right across those regularities. It was by a miraculously provided route across the Red Sea that the Israelites escaped from slavery in Egypt, and it was by similar miraculous means that they crossed the Jordan into their promised land. And even if we allow these, and other such dramatic events that appear on the pages of the Old Testament, to be the rich embellishments of later story-telling, it is still difficult to see how God's hand could have played the determinative role ascribed to it. Were all the many people, inside and outside the nation, who played key parts in Israel's destiny, really having their hearts softened or hardened by God, like Pharaoh, so that what seemed to be the practical decisions of power-hungry emperors or generals were at a deeper level due to the overruling of God in the interest of a higher, divine purpose? Such a notion may not be logically impossible, but it seems hardly compatible with the way in which we all normally set about making sense of the tangled story of human history.

But if the difficulty of rendering the notion of God's providential control of the vicissitudes of history intelligible is not in itself decisive evidence against such a notion, there is a fourth difficulty of a very different kind. So far it might seem that any Christian must *want* to hold on to a belief in God's providential care of the world and of individual people in it. Isn't such a notion at the heart of any faith that will really make a difference to the life of our world and to our own lives as individuals within it? Of what concern would God be to us if God has no impact on the way the world goes? Could I speak of God's love for me personally if God does not act specifically in response to my needs and to my prayers? Those are questions we will have to face. But for the moment we need to recognize that there is also what I will call a moral difficulty implicit in the idea that God *does* exercise providential control of the world. It is this. If God can determine the fate of nations and meet the needs of individuals, whether by miraculous intervention or by other means, to the degree that the Bible suggests and that Christian faith has usually taught, why were those divine powers not used to prevent such major tragedies as Auschwitz or Hiroshima? If the notion of specific divine action in the world is an intelligible one, and one that we affirm to have been at work in Christian history, then there is a moral difficulty we have to face about such occurrences as the Holocaust, where we stand abashed by what appears to be its callous absence. The daunting problem that already waits in store for us of how we are to account for the horrendous evil in the world is made even more intractable if it is really the case that God controls what happens in our history and determines, sometimes by miraculous means, the outcome of particular events.

I began this section by reflecting on some early Old Testament stories, and it may seem that I have been making an unnecessary amount of fuss about them. Much of what Christians value in the Old Testament, it might be argued, would still be available for them to draw on, even if we set on one side its understanding of God's control of history as the outmoded belief of a past age. But for Christians the Old Testament is, among other things, that which provides the setting for the New. It provides the context for the understanding of the life and mission of Jesus, which is incontrovertibly central to Christian faith. And it is precisely the understanding of God's providential guidance of history, with miraculous events at key moments within it, that shapes the telling of the story of Jesus in the New Testament. His coming into the world is seen as the fulfilling climax to that providential history, and his birth, his ministry and his death are all marked by strikingly miraculous occurrences. I deliberately began with the Old Testament, where it is easier for Christians to acknowledge the difficulty inherent in the notions of providence and miracle. But I also entitled the section 'The God of the Bible' rather than 'the God of the Old Testament', because that same difficulty is present in the New Testament as well. So the next step is to consider in more detail how it affects the New Testament account of Jesus and the traditional Christian understanding of him.

Interlude II: Using the Bible

From the start I have been talking about the Bible and the understanding of God to be found there. That was natural enough, as it is problems inherent in Christian belief that I am trying to deal with in this book, and the Bible has been central to Christian belief and religious life down the ages. But before we take that investigation any further, we need to consider what sort of a book the Bible is.

I speak of it as 'a book', because that is how it comes to us – a single volume between two hard or limp covers. But the Greek word from which 'Bible' comes is a plural form meaning 'the books'. The Bible is, in fact, a collection of books, the work of many different authors, written over many centuries and in more than one language. So large a temporal and cultural span should lead us to expect a variety of standpoints. And that is what we find. To take only one obvious example: the God who commands the ethnic cleansing of the existing inhabitants of Canaan, so that it can serve as the promised land where the children of Israel's ways of worship will be uncontaminated by the idolatry of those around them, is a very different God from the one who commands us to love our enemies.

The Bible also comes to us as a holy book, different from all other books in the status ascribed to it and in the way in which it is read. That is true to the role the church has given it down the ages. But it was not self-evident to the church from the outset which books deserved to be included among the biblical writings. That was a process that took time. There was no great problem about the composition of the Old Testament. The books that we know as the Apocrypha, works written in Greek rather than Hebrew in the centuries shortly before the birth of Christ, were generally included – as they still are by the

Roman Catholic Church, though at the time of the Reformation Protestants gave them a secondary status, and today they are to be found included in some Bibles but not in others. It was with the New Testament that there was the greatest uncertainty. The general shape of its contents emerges towards the end of the second century. The special status of the four Gospels, for example, is clear by then. But other books, like Revelation, remained questionable in the eyes of many church leaders for a lot longer. The first time that we meet with a list of New Testament books exactly as we have it now is in the second half of the fourth century, and it was a good deal later still before this was a matter of general agreement. Nor for the most part were the books written with a view to serving as Scripture; they were written for some specific, immediate purpose, and later taken over to serve a larger scriptural role. Most of Paul's letters, for example, which figure so prominently in the New Testament, were not written as careful expositions of the gospel but were passionate attempts to meet some current crisis in a local church community. Furthermore some biblical books are based on earlier ones and are not afraid to make substantial changes to them. The author of the books of Chronicles, for example, draws on the earlier books of Samuel and Kings, but alters them a good deal in order to tell a rather different story. In the New Testament, Matthew and Luke both made use of Mark's Gospel in composing their own. But they didn't treat it as 'gospel truth'; they had no hesitation in altering parts of what it said.

So it is not surprising that we meet with a bewildering variety, and sometimes a direct contradiction, of views within the Bible. The books of Ezra and Ruth, for example, take directly opposed views on the question of marriage between Jews and non-Jews. Or again, the Fourth Gospel presents a very different account of the nature of Christ, the style of his preaching and the content of his message from that given by any of the other three evangelists. And so one could go on. But that may suffice to illustrate the fundamental point. The teaching of the Bible is not uniform; and a lot of it applies to conditions very different from our own. So if it is to teach us about God and to be a guide to our conduct, it cannot do so in any simple or straight-forward way. Difficult questions of interpretation are bound to arise, and there are no short cuts.

Theoretical discussions of interpretation (or 'hermeneutics', to give them their more technical name) are a prominent feature of contemporary culture, and show a wide spectrum of differing views. At one end of the spectrum is the more old-fashioned view (known as 'authorial intention') according to which the goal of the interpreter is to discover the original intention of the author; at the other is the radically subjective view (known as 'reader response') which stresses the independent existence of the text and puts all its weight on how the reader reacts to it. Neither is very convincing in so extreme a form. Is it really possible to penetrate the intention of a sometimes unknown author, distant from us in age and culture? And, on the other hand, texts are surely not so pliable that they can properly be said to mean whatever we make of them? The truth of the matter must lie somewhere between the two extremes. It must involve a meeting between the intended or received meaning of the text in its original context and the different mind-set of its contemporary readers. That process can be a creative one. At its best a new vision of truth may emerge – larger than anything seen by the original author and at the same time correcting and deepening the understanding of the reader.

Christians often speak of the Bible as 'the Word of God'. Sometimes that is understood in an almost literal sense, as if the Bible contained words whose absolute and unchanging truth is guaranteed because they come in a uniquely direct way from God. But the nature of the Bible, as I have so briefly described it, rules out any such interpretation of the phrase. It needs to be understood in a much looser sense as affirming that the Bible, despite all its imperfections and inconsistencies, is an important medium through which we can still find a vital source for a knowledge of God. But we cannot do so by simply taking over what it says about God or about Jesus. It is not that that is a possibility we choose to reject; in a world in which human knowledge is always on the move it is just not possible to take over the meaning of an ancient text in so direct a way.

But through the creative process of interpretation that I have indicated, the Bible can enter into dialogue with our contemporary understanding and help to give rise to a specifically Christian vision of the world. And one inescapable part of that process is the kind of critical investigation of its teaching on which we have embarked, and which we must continue to pursue.

3

Son of God

*What does it mean to call
Jesus God?*

So what is 'the traditional Christian understanding of Jesus'?
The Apostles' Creed, the simplest and most basic form of the
Christian creed, is the natural place to turn for an answer.

> I believe in Jesus Christ his only Son our Lord, who was
> conceived by the Holy Ghost, born of the Virgin Mary,
> suffered under Pontius Pilate, was crucified, dead, and
> buried; he descended into Hell; the third day he rose again
> from the dead, he ascended into heaven, and sitteth on the
> right hand of God the Father Almighty; from thence he
> shall come to judge the quick and the dead.

The most striking thing about that account of what Christians
believe about Jesus Christ is that there is no mention of his
life or his ministry or his teaching. The old nursery rhyme
about Solomon Grundy, who was 'born on Monday, christ-
ened on Tuesday, married on Wednesday, took ill on Thurs-
day, worse on Friday, died on Saturday, buried on Sunday',
does at least include one mention of the period between the
events surrounding his birth and those leading up to his death.
But in the case of Jesus Christ there is nothing in between;
we move straight from the one to the other. This is partly
because the early creeds concentrated on matters that were
in dispute between Christians, and his ministry and teaching
were not controversial, as were questions about who he was
and about the manner of his coming into the world and of

his leaving it. But that was not the main reason. The main reason was that those latter questions were felt to be of far greater importance for Christian faith. The centrality of Jesus for faith derived from the distinctive nature of his person and from what he achieved for humankind by the sheer facts of his birth, his death and his resurrection. That provided the heart of the Christian story and the heart of the Christian faith.

The two questions – 'who was Jesus?' and 'what are the significance of his birth and death for us?' – are closely tied up with one another. The meaning of the Christian story, as it finds expression in the three moments of birth, death and resurrection highlighted in the Apostles' Creed, can be spelt out something like this: the birth or incarnation of Jesus bridges a gap between the transient world of our ordinary, day-to-day existence and the unchanging world of God's perfection; the death of Jesus breaks the barrier between those two worlds that has been created by human wrong-doing and sin; and the resurrection overcomes the one inexorable fate of all human life, namely the certainty and finality of death. But those events only have that significance because of who Jesus is, because he was not only a member of the human race but also, in the words of the Creed, 'God's only Son'. What are we to make of that story?

Before we try to determine how best to understand the story as a whole, we need to look in a little more detail at each of its component parts.

What does it mean to speak of Jesus as *Son of God*? That the language is not to be taken literally hardly needs saying. But in the earliest days of the church it did need saying. The Greek gods had many sons by means of liaisons with mortal women. Zeus, for example, was the father of Herakles by Alkmene, of Minos by Europa and many more besides. Jesus was not a son of God in that sense. The background to the term was Jewish rather than Greek. In the Old Testament both the people of Israel as a whole and the king in particular as representative of the people were spoken of as 'son of

God'. (The prophet Hosea describes the Exodus and the establishment of Israel as a nation with words spoken by God, 'Out of Egypt I called my Son'; and the prophet Nathan assures David that the royal line will be secured through Solomon by delivering God's promise, 'I will be a father to him and he will be my son'.) On the divine side the term implied that Israel owed its very existence as a people to God's choice of them and special favour towards them; they were the 'chosen' people, or heirs in God's household. And on the human side it implied an ideal of perfect obedience to the will and commands of God, though with appropriate hopes and expectations. (Complete obedience was seen as a much more fundamental characteristic of being a son then than it is today.) It was those two ideas that were at the root of what was implied in speaking of Jesus as Son of God. On the one hand he is 'the beloved Son in whom God is well pleased' that the voice at his baptism declares him to be; and on the other he is the Son who always does his Father's will, even when that will can only be embraced through the agony of the Garden of Gethsemane and the suffering of the cross.

To say further that Jesus is not only 'Son of God' but 'God's *only* Son' is to affirm that he is these things in some quite unique way. But what constitutes that uniqueness? In the early days different Christian groups did not all understand it in the same way. The evidence is far from straightforward, and there is plenty of scope for divergent interpretations of it. Modern scholarly accounts have taken full advantage of that scope and read the story in a variety of different ways. What is clear is that as the movement grew, there was increasing pressure to find a common, agreed account, and with the coming of Constantine and the new positive links between church and state that pressure became unstoppable. So the Ecumenical Councils of the fourth and fifth centuries laid down and enforced more precise definitions. To call Christ Son of God, decreed the Council of Nicaea (AD 325), meant that he was 'of one substance with the Father'. In other words, he was not just an agent or messenger of God, no matter how much greater than earlier prophets or deliverers. As only Son he shared God's essential nature; he was in his own person God, in the same sense that the Father was God. And that, as the Council of Chalcedon (AD 451) insisted, must not be thought to undermine his human status. Just as he was God in the same full sense that the Father is, so also he was human in the same full sense that we are. How full divinity and full humanity were combined in the one person of Jesus Christ was not made clear. In the years that followed, the church continued to be torn by debates as to how that could be the case: did Christ, for example, have two distinct wills or just one? Modern reflection on what is involved in being a human person has done nothing to make the concept any easier to understand. What above all led the church to come to that decision (a process which cost a great deal of ink and blood) was the conviction that only that understanding of Jesus could account for the radical transformation of life that Christians experienced through his birth, death and resurrection. But before taking these reflections any further, a little more needs to be said about the nature of those creeds which we have taken as our starting-point for Christian belief about Christ and then about those moments in the story which are picked out by the creeds as of special importance for faith.

Interlude III: Creeds

The two best-known forms of creed, accepted by almost all major Christian bodies, are the Apostles' Creed (used in the Anglican baptism service and at Morning and Evening Prayer) and the Nicene Creed (used at eucharistic services). Both derive from early baptismal creeds, and it was the rite of baptism, at which converts publicly affirmed their allegiance to their new faith, that provided the initial context for the emergence of creeds.

Despite its name and early legends, the Apostles' Creed was not composed by the apostles, nor does it date back to the time of the apostles. Indeed, in the precise form in which we now have it, it dates back only to the eighth century. But very similar forms were in use in Italy in the fourth century; and very similar words in an interrogatory rather than declaratory form (that is to say, spoken by the officiant at a baptism in the form of a question, to which those being baptized gave their assent, rather than a set of words recited by the new converts themselves) can be traced back as far as second-century Rome.

The Nicene Creed derives from the Council of Constantinople in AD 381, a somewhat similar form having been adopted earlier at the Council of Nicaea in AD 325. It is based on an Eastern baptismal creed, but was adapted at the Council to serve the rather different function of ensuring the orthodoxy of bishops, who were both the leaders of the church and the principal teachers of the faith. The aim of both councils was to guard against contemporary forms of teaching that were regarded as heretical, in particular against the 'Arian' heresy, which did affirm Christ to be divine, but in some lesser sense than that in which the Father was God. To that end Christ, as we have already seen, was defined not simply as 'God's only

Son' but more specifically as being 'of one substance with the Father'. The Nicene Creed was not originally designed for use in eucharistic worship, but it began to be so used in the East in the fifth century; in Rome, however, the practice was not adopted until the beginning of the second millennium.

It is clear from this account of how our creeds grew up that their initial purpose was to express what was distinctive about true Christian faith, over against other forms of belief – Jewish, Graeco-Roman or what were regarded as deviant forms of Christianity. It was not a compendium of everything a Christian believed or lived by. In the very early days of the church the precise wording used was not considered important and varied from place to place. Many pressures were at work in moving the church towards ever more precise and more uniform formulation of the creeds. Most prominent among them was the urge of ecclesiastical, and still more political, authorities to exercise greater control over the churches within their domains. It is no coincidence that it was the emperor Constantine, seeking to bring unity to an empire recently divided by a long period of civil war, who presided over the Council of Nicaea; that it was Theodosius I who was insistent that the Council of Constantinople should free the empire of the divisions brought about by conflict between orthodoxy and heresy; and that it was Charlemagne who secured the monopoly of the final form of the Apostles' Creed as part of his imperial reforms.

But important as ecclesiastical and political pressures were, the credal forms adopted were not simply imposed from above. They grew out of the church's continuing attempt to articulate its faith more clearly for its work of teaching and preaching. Despite the outside pressures and internal rivalries that influenced the councils at which they were formally adopted, they were also the fruit of devoted study, reflection and prayer. But like the Scriptures, the creeds are inevitably the children of their age. The precise understanding of the faith that they embody is affected by the way in which Scripture was then understood and by the particular problems besetting the church at the time. So while they serve a valuable purpose as expressions of a continuity in the structure of Christian faith down the ages, the story of their development and also of their use (and abuse) for political ends in the ensuing centuries is a reminder that we need to use them as guides to our critical reflection and not as answers to our questions. Their continued use in contemporary worship is better seen as a sign of our solidarity with Christians of past ages than as a quasi-legal requirement of what we should believe if we are to share in the life of the church today.

4

Birth, Death and Resurrection

Did they all really happen?

The story of Jesus' *birth* is told in only two of the four Gospels. In both cases, Matthew and Luke, the first two chapters, in which that story is told, have a different feel to them from the rest of the Gospel; the prominent role of angels as messengers from God in both accounts is just one of a number of features that serve to convey the atmosphere of story-telling or of legend. There is nothing very surprising about that. It is not uncommon for ancient biographies to begin in that way. Only in the case of hereditary monarchs is a person's birth likely to be a part of public history from the start. Usually it is only many years later, when the person concerned has made his or her mark in the world, that interest in the events surrounding that person's birth arises. And by that time reliable knowledge is often hard to come by. In the ancient world generally, stories of the birth of those who later achieved greatness are often marked by appropriate tales of a miraculous or legendary character. In the Old Testament, for example, the births of Isaac and of Samuel are explicitly foretold to women who have long given up all hope of conceiving a child, in Sarah's case indeed, to a woman well past the age of child-bearing. Such tales are a way of conveying in vivid story form the great significance of the child in the purposes of God for the nation or for the world. It is in the context of that tradition that we need to approach the two accounts of Jesus' birth.

When we look more carefully at them, it is surprising to discover how little they have in common. In Matthew's account it is wise men or astrologers from a great distance who come to pay homage to Jesus; according to Luke it is local shepherds. In Matthew's version of the story the holy family only goes to Nazareth because it is still too dangerous to go back to their old home at Bethlehem when they return from the exile in Egypt to which Herod's savagery had driven them; according to Luke, Nazareth had always been the family home and Jesus was only born in Bethlehem because his parents had to go there to register for a Roman census. One thing they do have in common is that Jesus was conceived virginally and not by the normal means of sexual intercourse. It can be argued that this agreement at the heart of two such different accounts points to it as the nub of historical truth at the root of the two stories. But, even apart from the difficulties that attach to so miraculous a claim, it seems more natural to take it as the common core of a characteristic tale of the kind that so often grew up around the birth of a great hero. Certainly the telling of the story was much influenced by impressive tales from the Old Testament, such as those that describe the births of Isaac and Samuel in ways designed to bring out the direct involvement of God in such momentous events.

The Virgin Birth does not, however, seem to have played any central role in the faith of the earliest Christians. It receives no clear mention in any other writing of the New Testament. It was probably not very widely known at first. When we do first meet with explicit reference to it in the second century, it is appealed to as evidence not of Jesus' divine nature, but rather of the surprising fact that a divine saviour should actually have been born of a human mother. But it was not long before all that was to change. As time went on, the Virgin Birth came to be seen as an essential prerequisite for Jesus to have been the saviour that Christian faith proclaimed him to be. That deeply felt conviction was given a variety of theoretical explanations. Contemporary ideas of procreation stressed the role of the male seed, seeing the woman's role in purely receptive terms; so the absence of a human father brought out the absolute priority of God's action in the coming of Jesus into the world. Or again there was a deep-seated distrust of sex, more in the Hellenistic world which was the milieu in which the early church grew up than in the Jewish world out of which it had emerged; and this gave rise to the view that only one born without the contamination that sexual intercourse involved could be free of the taint of sin inherited from Adam and so able to fulfil the role of a saviour from sin. So the Virgin Birth, once established as an unquestioned feature of the Christian creed, became a focus not only of what the church believed about Christ, but of many other things as well: conceptions of God's grace; ideals of womanhood; and attitudes to sex.

By contrast, the story of Christ's *death* is the climax of each Gospel and central to the earliest Christian preaching. Nor is its historical character in question. Plenty of questions still surround the details of the story – Was it the leading Jews or the occupying Romans who were primarily responsible for bringing it about? What was it about the message or activity of Jesus that provoked such violent hostility? – but the fact itself is not in doubt. However, bare facts (if such things exist!) are of no great interest apart from their significance; it is what they are understood to mean that gives them their importance. And here there is a marked contrast once again with the Virgin Birth. Whatever we today may make of the notion of a virginal conception and birth, there were many at the time to whom it seemed appropriate to a divine figure. But death by crucifixion, the death of a common criminal, could hardly be less fitting. It was unthinkable that someone worthy of divine honour should have died in such a way. Indeed the Old Testament, as Paul acknowledges, could be taken to imply the exact opposite – namely that Jesus was the object of God's disfavour, that God's curse rested on him. Familiarity may make us fail to recognize the striking nature of the Christian response to so natural an objection. So, far from being inappropriate to his divine role, the death of Jesus on the cross, they claimed, was the heart of God's always intended purpose in the sending of Jesus into the world. It was God's loving gift to humankind, providing a remedy for sin and guilt, an antidote to the apparently inescapable finality of death, and (somewhat less prominently) a source of strength and comfort in the universal phenomenon of human suffering. Once again there were a variety of theoretical accounts of how it achieved those ends, drawing, for example, on contemporary ideas of sacrifice. But it was the fact of Christ's death and the power of its effects rather than how those effects were brought about that was central – even though much later in the church's life some of those explanations have on occasion come to be regarded as absolute and unquestionable truths.

None of these benefits were the fruit of Christ's death alone; they were the fruit of Christ's death and *resurrection*. The death and resurrection of Christ were not so much two stories as two parts of a single story. And it is in the climax of the story, which tells of Christ's resurrection, that for many people today the most difficult questions reside. For it shares the radically miraculous character that marks the story of the Virgin Birth, but combines it with the same centrality to Christian faith and preaching that appertains to the story of his crucifixion. It was the reversal of the crucifixion and the necessary basis for giving a positive interpretation to Christ's death.

But what exactly was this 'resurrection' of Jesus that was so central to Christian affirmation? It was not just a return to the life he had before; it was not a raising to life in the same sense as that portrayed in the Gospel stories of the raising of Lazarus, Jairus' daughter or the widow of Nain's son. It was a moving into a new form of life, altogether beyond death. Our earliest account of it comes not in any of the Gospels but in Paul's first letter to the Corinthians, written about twenty years after the time of Jesus. In that letter Paul speaks of a series of appearances to the disciples and others, the sequence culminating in a belated and exceptional appearance to himself, thus aligning Paul's own much later, visionary experience on the Damascus Road with the appearances to the disciples in the days immediately following the death of Jesus. The Gospels, written some decades after Paul's letter to the Corinthians, speak first of the discovery of an empty tomb and the disappearance of the body of Jesus, with attendant angels to help the disciples understand their significance. The earliest Gospel, Mark, which originally ended at chapter 16 verse 8, stops there and says nothing about any appearance of Jesus. The accounts the other Gospels do go on to give of his appearances to the disciples vary not only in incidental detail of place and time, but also in the nature of what they affirm. In Luke and John the risen Jesus appears in a locked room and vanishes again from sight; but he also eats a piece of fish to show that he has flesh and bones (Luke), and invites Thomas to thrust his hand into his pierced side (John). Even if we were to set on one side the difficulties that the radically miraculous character of the records pose for us and to regard ourselves as bound to accept the teaching of the texts in its most straightforward sense (which I have already argued would in fact be a most inappropriate and unreasonable procedure!), it would be hard to know just what that teaching was with respect to the nature of Jesus' resurrection as a historical happening. The stories are patently not straightforward historical records themselves, and they do not readily yield answers to questions about just what it was that happened, even when we take careful account of their genre and their context.

Ideas of resurrection appear only at a comparatively late stage in the development of Jewish faith that the Old Testament depicts. The Psalmist's anguished cry to God that 'in death there is no remembrance of thee' is representative of the expectation of the great majority of the people of Israel in the period before Christ. Where hope of resurrection did begin to take hold shortly before the time of Christ, it was in the context of hopes for God's final vindication of Israel that flowered in times of severe persecution. It took the form of hope for a general resurrection at the end of history as we know it rather than the resurrection of each individual at death. So the resurrection of Jesus was seen as a prelude to the final completion of God's purposes for humankind, a foretaste of what his followers could look forward to sharing with him. Meanwhile they could enjoy a risen quality of life in Christ here and now in the period before the end. All this rich, religious meaning has coloured the way the stories of Jesus' own resurrection were told and used within the life of the church. Attempts to determine a historical core at the root of the stories as we now have them – either in terms of a historical event involving some miraculous resuscitation of the dead body of Jesus or in more mundane terms of, for example, a mistaken tomb or hallucinatory appearances – are no more than unsubstantiated guesses. The evidence is simply not of a kind to enable us to reach a reasoned judgment.

There are three further moments in the story of Christ as the creed affirms it: his *ascension,* his *sitting at the right hand of God* and his future *coming to judge the quick and the dead.* These need not detain us very long. For most people today they do not give rise to such intensity of questioning and doubt as the stories of Christ's birth and resurrection. That is not because we can more readily accept them in their straightforward surface meaning. Rather the opposite. They seem so patently to belong to the realm of symbolic story that it does not seriously occur to us to take them in any other way. Moreover they seem so much less central to Christian faith that the whole question appears to be one of far less importance.

There may be much truth in all that, but it is not quite the end of the matter. Most New Testament writers who refer to the *ascension* do not differentiate it from the resurrection. It is only Luke who treats it as a separate incident, with its own story at an interval of forty days from the resurrection. It is Luke's account that has established itself in the general consciousness of the church, because it fitted so well the needs of liturgical remembrance where the spacing out in time helps the church to follow in the steps of Christ in its regular cycle of worship. But whether the ascension is seen as a separate occasion or not, its message is the same: it is one that we have already noted, namely that Christ's resurrection was not a return to his former life but a transition to a new form of life, with God.

To speak of *sitting at the right hand of God* involves a more vivid use of human imagery than most of the language about God that has taken root in the thought and worship of the church. The phrase, derived from the Psalms, underlines the message of the ascension: the life of the risen Christ is not only a new form of life, life with God; it is a life that shares in the honour and dignity of God's being.

A future *coming to judge the quick and the dead* has often been understood to imply a literal reversal of a literally understood ascension. Such expectations, indeed, are not dead and will no doubt flourish at the forthcoming end of this millennium. But however easily we may feel able to dismiss such expectations as delusory, the presence of the phrase in the creed is not so easily dealt with. Not only has it loomed very large through most of Christian history, it is more central to the coherence of Christian faith than might at first sight appear to be the case. The way of God revealed in Christ, it affirms, is the standard by which the world will be judged and its ultimate destiny be determined. Even if we are confident that that will not be achieved by way of a literal return of Christ to this earth, we are faced with the question: is there *any* way in which the underlying conviction of that hope might conceivably be fulfilled?

This brief survey of the final three moments in the credal telling of the story of Christ may serve to remind us of two things:

1. These aspects of the creed seem unquestionably to call for a highly symbolic form of understanding, even though they have normally been understood in more literal ways in the past. It is not, therefore, a very surprising move to suggest that some other aspects of Christian belief ought to be treated in a more symbolic way than has been customary within the church.

2. Recognizing the symbolic character of our beliefs often frees us from particular forms of doubt and difficulty that assail us if we feel under an obligation to take them in a more straightforward or literal way. But it is no magic charm for removing all doubt and difficulty from Christian belief. We still have to ask what it is that the various facets of the Christian story symbolize, what it is towards which they point. And then we have to judge whether we have good grounds to accept that the direction in which they point is one that we ought to follow.

Interlude IV: Miracles

Miracles are widely regarded as epitomizing the supposed conflict between religion and science. Certainly miracles, as we have seen, figure prominently in the Bible; yet they have no place in the working assumptions of the practising scientist. That doesn't amount to saying that they are central to the life of faith, but impossible for any scientist to accept. There is an obvious conflict, but it isn't as straightforward as that. So it is worth exploring a bit more thoroughly what is involved.

The main problem in making any general statement about the possibility or impossibility of miracles is the difficulty of defining precisely what a miracle is. A strong version might go something like: 'a direct act of God that contravenes the laws of nature'. But 'laws of nature' is a slippery concept. What we call 'laws of nature' are not absolute rules from which any deviation is known to be impossible. They are generalizations drawn from experience of the regularities of nature as we have observed and codified them. But they are constantly being modified and revised. Newton's laws of physics proved not to hold in all circumstances, and had to be revised in the light of relativity theory. Revisions of that sort are the stuff of which progress in science is made. On this strong definition of miracle it soon becomes clear that we can't always be sure whether an occurrence ought to be classified as a miracle or not. A purported miracle may conflict with the laws of nature as we now understand them, but those laws may themselves turn out to be in need of revision. So we may be tempted to try in its place a weaker definition such as: 'a highly remarkable occurrence of profound religious significance'. We would certainly be able to find happenings that fit such a description, but not all of them would be of a kind that we would normally describe as a 'miracle'.

What our two suggested definitions have in common is that each of them incorporates both a scientific and a religious dimension. And that is an essential feature of any satisfactory definition of miracle: it must include reference to the unusual character of the event in relation to the normal way things happen and also to its supernatural origin or religious importance. So having acknowledged our inability to produce a satisfactory and watertight definition (a common enough experience in many areas of discussion), we can best pursue our enquiry by reflecting further on those two dimensions of the concept of miracle.

Strange things do happen. Some of them seem to run counter not only to what we had expected, but also to what we had, up till then, assumed to be universal regularities. If such a happening is of a kind that can be repeated, we repeat it – several times if necessary. If the same unexpected result continues to recur, we conclude that what we had taken to be universal laws need to be revised; if it does not, we conclude that we must have been mistaken in our initial observation. But happenings of deep religious significance are unlikely to be of a kind that can be repeated, and are therefore not open to that kind of checking. The most natural response in such cases is to assume that the initial event must have been wrongly observed or misdescribed in some way. The case for making such an assumption is not, of course, as strong as it is where it has been possible to repeat the conditions of the original occurrence. But it is strong nonetheless, especially when our source of knowledge of the supposed miraculous event is not, as is often the case, direct observation but a record from the distant past. If there are independent grounds for affirming belief in God (as I have suggested there are) and if the purported miracle can be shown to fit with other knowledge about the nature of God, the concept of ascribing the miraculous event to direct divine action is a possible explanation that cannot simply be dismissed as logically incoherent. But the evidence to move us beyond, at most, a suspension of judgment about the true nature of the event would have to be very strong indeed. We need therefore to ask whether the case for accepting the reality of miracles, generally thought to be an essential ingredient in Christian faith, is of the strength that would be required.

What then are the grounds in Christian faith for affirming the reality of miracle? We have already noted their plentiful presence in the Bible, and the implications of that fact must be taken into account. But more significant is the further question: how crucial is the role played by miracle in Christian faith as a whole?

All the biblical writings derive from times when accounts of miracles were a much more common feature of the surrounding culture than they are today. It is not, of course, the case that people then were unaware of the regularities that characterize the way things happen in the world. Indeed without such recognition the concept of miracle cannot arise. But they had much less understanding of how, underlying those evident regularities, there is a complex range of further interlocking regularities which are not themselves open to the naked eye but which subsequent scientific study has been able to disclose. In the absence of such more detailed knowledge, relatively rare occurrences, like an eclipse or an earthquake, can only appear as baffling departures from the normal way of things; to ascribe them to some supernatural cause was a natural enough reaction. So there is nothing very exceptional in the presence of miracle stories in the Bible. Many of them are of a clearly legendary character, and have no claim to be treated as accurate accounts of what happened. I have already argued that this applies even to some miracle stories, like the Virgin Birth, that have come to play a prominent role in later Christian belief. So the mere presence of miracle stories in the Bible is not in itself the kind of strong evidence that would be needed to make us consider seriously the possibility that some particular events may cut across all the normal regularities that science either has disclosed or will disclose in the future, and are to be ascribed to the direct action of God. For miracle stories to affect us in that way, they would at the very least have not merely to figure in the biblical record but also to be an indispensable element in Christian faith as a whole.

There is no denying the fact that miracle has been intimately tied up with the history of Christian belief. One may perhaps distinguish three main roles that miracles have played. In the first place miracles, particularly the resurrection, have often been used as evidence designed to prove the truth of Christian faith. That has never been the main line of argument for the truth of Christian claims, but it has played a part in such arguments. However, any such appeal to miracle has serious obstacles to overcome. We have already seen how difficult it is to determine whether or not a miracle has taken place; and even if it has, the genuineness of the occurrence is likely to be as much open to doubt as the belief for which it is supposed to be the decisive evidence. Moreover such a use of miracle is religiously questionable. One frequently repeated element in the recorded teaching of Jesus himself was a refusal to accede to requests to provide a miraculous sign as evidence of the divine authority for his teaching.

Another very different way in which miracle has been seen as important to faith is as an expression of God's personal love and care for his children. If there is to be the kind of personal relationship between God and the believer that is central to the experience of much Christian faith, it is argued, must not that relationship find expression in divine response to human prayers as well as in human prayer to God? And if those responses are genuinely responses to human requests, must they not often involve direct divine intervention which alters what would otherwise have happened? The difficulties attendant on the practice of petitionary and intercessory prayer is something to which we must return later, but there are serious problems in seeing miracle as integral to their solution. Miracles by definition must be relatively rare; otherwise the degree of regularity that science has been able to disclose would not appertain and would not have been there to be discovered. And if miracle is necessarily an exceptional event, it can hardly be crucial to so basic and regular a feature of Christian life as prayer. Moreover there is a further difficulty about prayers that are not answered. If divine response of a miraculous kind is a genuine possibility and a feature of the regular life of prayer, there is a puzzle about the kinds of happening that are often claimed as answers to prayer and the kinds of prayer, perhaps about much more grievous ills, that apparently go unanswered. The deeper the exploration into the practice of prayer, the less helpful does the concept of miracle appear. So, far from providing the strong support needed to overcome the serious difficulties that scientific knowledge puts in the way of accepting the possibility of miracle, this consideration of the religious dimension indicates that on that score also there are grounds for misgiving about the concept of miracle.

The third role that miracle has played in traditional faith is the most general and fundamental. Miracle, it may be claimed, is integral to the substance of the faith. Without miracle (and again particularly the miracle of the resurrection) the faith would not so much lack proof; it would lack existence. For only direct divine action, going right against the most fundamental regularity of the irreversibility of human death, would be strong enough to bring about those basic realities of Christian faith – the forgiveness of sins and the promise of eternal life. The only way of resolving that issue is to see whether there is a way of stating the main substance of Christian faith which does not depend on any such directly miraculous occurrence. And that brings us back to the point that our main discussion had just reached. If the story of Christ as it has been traditionally affirmed in the creed calls for the degree of question and revision that I have been suggesting, does it remain a gospel by which men and women may continue to live and worship today? It is to that question that we must now return.

5

The Christian Story

Is it true?

We began this section of our discussion by taking the Apostles' Creed as a summary of traditional belief about Jesus. We then looked very briefly at some of the particular affirmations that are central to that belief. While there is much more that could be said on either side of the debates about the issues involved, I have felt bound to acknowledge that there are some aspects of the beliefs spelt out in that creed that do not seem to fit happily either with the evidence that supposedly lies behind them or with the broader range of beliefs about the world that most of us share (and are convinced we are right to share) today. Such an admission is widely seen as incompatible with a continued acceptance of Christian faith. Is it possible to question the intelligibility of the traditional concept of Jesus as God-man, to regard the Virgin Birth as a legend and the bodily resurrection of Christ from the tomb as something of a similar character, and still profess oneself a believing Christian? Many will say 'No', but it is not the only answer that can be given.

What does it mean to ask about the 'truth' of a story? If a policeman asks the question he probably wants to assure himself of the accuracy of all the incidental details in the story he has been told; but if we use that sort of phrase in more everyday conversation and ask what the 'truth of the matter' really is, we will probably be looking for no more than a general reassurance about the overall reliability of the way the story in question has been told. Or take a pictorial example: a portrait, or even a caricature, can be 'truer' than a photo-

graph, if, as it often does, it communicates better the underlying personality of the one portrayed.

So in asking about the truth of the Christian story, we need
first to be clear about what the point of that story is and
about what the appropriate criteria for determining its truth-
fulness are. Even if a broadly literal understanding of the
Gospel accounts has been characteristic of the main Christian
tradition as a whole (and it has by no means been the universal understanding of the Christian mind down the ages), it
has still never been regarded as the sole, or even the most
important, aspect of Christian truth. Scriptural texts were
understood to have not only a literal but also a more important spiritual sense. However much the former might be
assumed, or even directly asserted, to be true, it was the latter
that mattered most. Christian truth is not simply about what
happened in the past; it is about God in his relation to the
present and the future, every bit as much as to the past.

We have already seen that in speaking about God, we can
in the nature of things speak only in indirect or symbolic
ways. That fact is crucial to any consideration of the 'truth'
of the Christian story. So our fundamental concern is not a
matter of the accuracy of historical detail about the life of
Jesus. Nor is it a matter of how closely we agree with the
way the Christian story has been understood and formally
summarized in the past. Continuity with the past, itself of
course containing a great deal of change and variety, is not
something to be dismissed out of hand as of no significance
for Christian faith, but it is continuity of a much broader
kind that matters. What is crucial is whether the story as we
understand it today still fulfils the role for which the church
has always primarily valued it, namely whether it points us
in the right direction for our understanding of and our
response to God. Putting it that way is not a case of making
do with a lesser degree of continuity than might have been
hoped for. Rather, the constant flow and massive extent of
historical and cultural change since the early days of Christianity and the necessarily indirect, symbolic character of all

language used of God combine to make it the appropriate kind of continuity to look for in the realm of religious belief.

So what basic convictions about God and the world underlie these traditional beliefs about Christ, by which the church has always sought to live? In trying to answer that question as best I can, I am not hoping to be able to come up with something on which everyone should be expected to agree. That would be inconsistent with what I have already said about the inevitably subjective character of all interpretation. But I am hoping to offer something which, however much people may want to add to it, would command a wide measure of assent.

I will set it out in the form of four brief statements:

1. The belief that Jesus Christ is the focal point of God's dealing with the world, which found formal expression in the doctrine of the incarnation, implies in the first place that the figure of Jesus should be of central significance in determining the content of our beliefs about God, our understanding of how our lives are meant to be lived, and the manner in which human lives can be transformed through faith in God.

2. That same belief also carries a more general implication; it symbolizes the intimacy of God's involvement with the world. If God has been seen as incarnate in a human life, then the primary way to a knowledge of God and the basic form of any relationship with God must come not by turning our backs on the world but by penetrating more deeply into its fundamental reality. It also carries with it important ethical implications of a positive nature about the value of the physical world.

3. The story of Jesus' death plays a crucial role in the impact that the figure of Jesus Christ has on our beliefs. It implies that unlimited self-giving love is at the heart of the nature of God; and that neither wickedness nor suffering can ever take us outside the range of God's presence. And in this aspect of the story too there are important ethical implications about the attitude to others which Christians are called to adopt.

4. The story of Christ's resurrection (which, as we have already seen, is really a part of the single story of death-and-resurrection) symbolizes the conviction that wickedness, suffering and death do not have the final word about human life. At an early stage in this discussion I drew a comparison between the form of the Apostles' Creed and the nursery rhyme about Solomon Grundy. But I did not quote the final phrase of the rhyme; after 'died on Saturday, buried on Sunday', it continues: 'This is the end of Solomon Grundy'. The resurrection story implies that that is not true of Jesus Christ or of human life more generally.

This way of expressing the symbolic significance of the Christian story by-passes a number of the difficulties that many people feel about it, particularly the miraculous character of some of its most prominent features. But even if it is broadly true that these should not be seen as the serious barriers to accepting Christian faith that they are so often taken to be, there are certainly other problems that this approach has to contend with. There are those who will see it as a very watered-down version of what they understand the traditional faith to be. But it is no humanist platitude, and certainly far from the scepticism that often vies with credulity for the souls of men and women today. It makes strong claims, some of which conflict with our common sense assumptions about the world.

In the chapters that follow I shall try to fill out these four brief and bald statements so that we can better see what they involve and better judge on what basis we might reasonably assent to them.

Interlude V: Symbolism

Symbolism is not, of course, a concept restricted to the sphere of religion, but one that plays an important role in many other spheres of life as well, such as art, literature and psycho-analysis. So what is meant by such terms as symbol, symbolism and symbolic truth, to which I have attached such importance for a proper understanding of Christian faith?

The exact meaning given to the terms varies a good deal between different disciplines and different writers. But a broad definition might go something like this.

Language refers to things in the world through a system of signs. A few Chinese characters are pictorial and have a visual resemblance to what they refer to, and a few words in most languages are onomatopoeic and indicate their meanings by their sounds. But for the great majority of words there is no organic relation between their form and their meaning; the link between the two is entirely conventional. In a good deal of our everyday communication and in much scientific work, we want our words to indicate what they refer to as unambiguously as possible. The carpet we need is *three* metres square, not *four*, the gas to be used is *oxygen*, not *hydrogen*. So the signs need to have clear and precise meanings with no fuzzy edges. But language does not function only to serve such specific and practical goals. It serves also to enlarge our horizons, to help us penetrate below the surface of our immediate sense experience. For those purposes language needs to be less narrowly defined. Its aim is not simply to enable us to identify what it refers to; it is designed also to help us see the thing it refers to in a new light, extending our appreciation of it by suggesting associations that would not otherwise have occurred to us or deepening our sense of its significance in ways that would not have been obvious without its help. When language functions like that, as it does in imaginative or poetic writing, we distinguish the way it is being used by speaking of it as involving the use of symbols rather than simply of signs. When we read in *Moby Dick* of Captain Ahab's relentless pursuit of the whale, the word 'whale' carries a far richer significance there than it does when it appears in a zoology textbook. The symbolic use of language is fundamental to culture in all its forms.

This symbolic use of language also plays an important role in establishing social cohesion and commitment. When demonstrators against a repressive authoritarian regime join in shouting 'Freedom!', they may have very varied conceptions of what that freedom would entail. The word 'freedom' in that context has no clearly defined meaning, but it may still serve as a powerful symbol which cements and deepens the joint commitment of those who chant it to a much needed goal that is incapable of more precise definition at that stage.

It is not only words, of course, that can function as symbols in that sort of way. Physical objects can also fulfil the same role. The national flag or a team mascot can recall and inspire strong sentiments of patriotic fervour or of some more local group loyalty. A bottle of wine shared with a stranger or a comrade does not only fulfil the biological role of quenching thirst; it can also remind us of and reinforce bonds of common humanity or close friendship. Lenin's tomb was a powerful symbol of the ideals of communist Russia. The bread of the eucharist incorporates a wide range of symbolic meaning: the given nature of those basic necessities whereby life is sustained; the sacrifical death of Christ on the cross; the sense of mutual belonging that should characterize a Christian community; and that community's common commitment to the service of the needy. Some of these symbols, like the national flag, are purely conventional, as almost all language is; some, like sharing a drink, have a natural link with what they express; some, like Lenin's tomb, are rooted in a past historical event; and some, like the eucharist, draw from both nature and history.

Historical events, particularly ones related to the founding of a nation, often take on a directly symbolic function, quite apart from their encapsulation in the form of some physical object or continuing ritual. Where a story from the past acquires such a symbolic role, it is often spoken of as a 'myth'. The myth of the founding of Rome, in a variety of forms involving Romulus and Aeneas, was a potent force in the early days of the expanding Roman empire; the myth of the Norman yoke fuelled the revolutionary attitudes of the under class in seventeenth-century Britain; and the Afrikaaner myth of the great trek gave the Afrikaaner people a strong sense of identity and of destiny. A long list of such myths could easily be compiled. In each case there are genuine historical events behind the stories; but the strength of the myth does not depend on the accuracy of the historical account. That may vary from the very slight to the substantial. What counts is the way the story is told, the hold it has on the imaginations of the people at large and its adaptability to meet the needs of the moment. The symbolic impact of such stories can be a powerful political reality.

What I have been trying to illustrate from a very disparate set of examples is the immense importance of symbols in human life. Most of the things that matter most to us, such as close family bonds or the appreciation of art and literature, cannot find adequate expression in the more straightforward forms of language use. A symbolic use of language is one of the main ways of giving expression to these deeper realities of life.

If symbolism is operative over such a wide range of human experience, it should be no matter for surprise that it plays a crucial role also in religious belief and practice, through which we seek to express our relation to the ultimate conditions of our existence. And just as symbols in general draw on the experience of both nature and history, so Christian affirmations about God are grounded in our responses to the natural world around us and also to the particular history out of which Christianity arose. In many of its most central tenets, symbolism of these two kinds is woven together in rich and complex ways. Thus the death and resurrection of Christ find their meaning not only in the historical events that marked the end of Jesus' life, but also in the annual cycle of the return of spring after winter. And the sacrament of baptism does not only re-enact that death and resurrection, as it did vividly in its original form with the person baptized being submerged under and coming up again out of the water, but draws also on the universal significance of water's cleansing power. Stressing the symbolic nature of the language of faith saves us from treating it as if it were on a par with ordinary, everyday, factual language and the misunderstandings of it to which that can give rise. It does not, of course, prove that it is true or beneficial; there can be evil symbols like the Nazi symbol of the Aryan race, and ill-founded symbols like the Marxist symbol of the proletarian revolution. The truth and worth of Christian faith are not vindicated simply by recognizing their symbolic character, but it is a vital first step towards such a goal to get a better understanding of the true nature of the claims that the faith makes.

6

Jesus

What can we really know
about him?

We have already noted in our reflections on the Apostles'
Creed that it says nothing about the course of Jesus' life, but
moves straight from his birth to his death; his character, his
teaching, his ministry of healing – none of these receives a
mention. And in my own summary of the Christian story,
the stress has still been firmly laid on the implications of his
birth, death and resurrection. But if my claim that 'the figure
of Jesus should be of central significance in determining the
content of our beliefs about God, our understanding of how
our lives are meant to be lived, and the manner in which
human lives can be transformed through faith in God' is to
be taken seriously, then the story of his life calls for more
attention than we have given it so far. What Jesus was like
as a person, what he taught and what he did must surely
be highly significant for Christian faith. Indeed in the late
nineteenth and early twentieth centuries it was widely felt
that a greater emphasis on the human life of Jesus, correcting
the one-sided traditional stress on his divine nature and the
saving acts of his birth, death and resurrection, might prove
to be a way of making Christian faith more relevant and
accessible to the concerns of men and women in the changed
world of a later age.

But the difficulties inherent in such a project should be
evident from what has already been said about the nature of
the Bible. The four Gospels are unquestionably the primary
source for our knowledge of the life of Jesus, and what was

said earlier about the Bible generally applies every bit as much to them as to any other part of it. So we have to face the questions: how much do we really know about the human life of Jesus? How well does such knowledge as may be available to us serve the needs of Christians today?

We know very little about how the Gospels came to be written or how they were first introduced into the life of the church. They were probably composed between about thirty-five and sixty-five years after Jesus' death. None of them was written by one of the original twelve disciples. Although the Gospels of Matthew and John bear the names of disciples, the evidence against apostolic authorship is overwhelming; it may be that in each case some of the traditions on which the Gospel draws go back to the teaching of the apostle whose name was then given to the work as a whole. But if there are such links, they don't seem to be very direct. Each of the Gospels, it would appear, was written to meet the needs of a particular congregation or group of congregations. The evangelists were not concerned to ensure historical accuracy, as a modern historian understands that phrase. Their aim was rather to present the traditions about Jesus that were known to them in a form appropriate to the situation of those for whom they were writing. With that purpose in view they were perfectly ready to modify or change the form of the tradition as they had received it. We can see that process at work in the way that Matthew and Luke, who both used Mark's Gospel in composing their own, felt free to alter what Mark had written. A similar process had no doubt been at work in the period (of some thirty to fifty years) during which the traditions were being handed on orally, before they came to be written down.

So it is hard to distinguish between what goes back to Jesus himself and what is the evangelist's adaptation of the story. But even if the historical questions could be answered with a good deal more certainty than seems possible now or likely to be possible in the future, it is not clear that it would be as valuable for faith as we might at first expect. The aim of

Jesus' ministry and the core of his teaching were directed to the situation and needs of those to whom he preached. To understand the significance of that ministry and teaching for us, we would need first to understand the needs and conditions of the time that elicited them. That we are able to do in part, but only to a limited degree. But even if we had a much more assured grasp of the aims of Jesus' ministry and a much deeper understanding of the precise intention of his actions and his teaching, there would still be scope for a great deal of variety in determining what their implications might be for our understanding of God or for the living of our lives in the very different world of today.

Does all this then undermine the value of the Gospels and of Jesus' life for Christian faith? It does undermine certain expectations that people often have about what the Gospel records of Jesus provide. We cannot be sure that the particular words ascribed to Jesus in the Gospels are words that he himself actually spoke. And that means that, whatever our belief about the divine nature of Jesus, we cannot ascribe to them the quality of unquestionable truth on the grounds that, as direct words of Jesus, they come to us with the imprint of an unmediated divine authority. But that was always an unrealistic expectation.

The nature of the Gospels as I have described them does not, on the other hand, preclude the words and actions of Jesus recorded there from having a more indirect, but more realistic role in the practice of Christian faith. Writing earlier about the Bible as a whole I said that 'through the creative process of interpretation . . . the Bible can enter into dialogue with our contemporary understanding and help to give rise to a specifically Christian vision of the world'. The Gospels are a part of the Bible particularly well suited to that role. However difficult it is to sort out the story of just how the Christian church emerged out of Judaism, there can be no question about Jesus being the primary source and focus of that movement from the outset. The Gospels, as we have seen, provide us with a picture of how the recollections of his life helped to form and guide the life of the early Christian communities – as well as enabling us to see how those recollections were themselves modified in the process. It is by a similar process that the Gospels can serve the needs of Christians today. For as we seek to interpret them in our own contemporary context, our reflections on the records of Jesus and the religious uses to which those records were put can contribute to the building up of our own Christian vision of the world.

I can best fill out that rather abstract account and illustrate how it might work out in practice by giving a brief, impressionistic account of my own reading of the figure of Jesus as presented in the Gospels. He stands out first and foremost as one for whom the God whom he calls Father is an ever-present and all-embracing reality. That is both a general truth ('all the hairs of your head are numbered' and 'not a sparrow falls to the ground without my Father') and also the basis of his own personal sense of mission which led him to speak with a note of such direct authority that it surprised his hearers and set him apart from the religious leaders of his day. This sense of God's presence and its overriding claim on him was not just a natural endowment; it was sustained by a life of prayer which entailed struggle and suffering, as the stories of Gethsemane ('Father, take away this cup from me; nevertheless not my will but thine be done') and the cry of dereliction on the cross ('My God, my God, why hast thou forsaken me?') bear witness.

The heart of his mission was to proclaim the coming of the kingdom, the present possibility of such a life of intimate and obedient relationship with God for all. Despite the directness of the authority with which he spoke, there was also an indirectness about the way in which his message was presented. The parables and the pithy proverbial sayings, which are the two most distinctive forms of his teaching, both have that oblique character which we have already seen to be an essential feature of all speech that is genuinely speech about God. Some of the parables end with the familiar phrase 'he who has ears to hear, let him hear'. A parable, that is to say, does not carry its meaning on the surface, plain for all to see. It achieves its aim only when it stimulates the imagination of the hearers, enabling them to assimilate its message and make something of it for themselves in their own way.

Something very similar seems to be true of the other main facet of Jesus' ministry – his work of healing. Whatever doubts we may legitimately have about the historical truth of many of the miracle stories, Jesus must at the very least have been a remarkable healer for such a cycle of stories to have grown up about him. But the healings are not presented in the Gospels simply as extraordinary cures. As acts of compassion and as exorcisms of demonic forces, they are symbols of the coming of God's kingdom, pictures of what is possible when the presence and authority of God are acknowledged. In a number of the healing stories Jesus' final word to the one healed is: 'Your faith has made you whole'. As the parables needed hearers who had 'ears to hear', so the healings needed patients with the imaginative trust that through Jesus their condition could be transformed. Whatever literal 'opening of the eyes of the blind' may or may not have marked Jesus' ministry of healing, the phrase vividly describes the transformation of human lives that took place as a result of his life and teaching.

It was not only the victims of physical disability who were the recipients of Jesus' ministry of healing. The records emphasize his close association with those called 'publicans and sinners' – men and women who for moral, social or religious reasons had been relegated to the margins of society. Jesus' acceptance of them was an expressive symbol of God's acceptance of them. That is a feature of the ministry that has close links with the fact of his death. It constituted a challenge to the conscientious concern for religious purity that was a characteristic of the religious leadership – then as so often before and since. If Jesus was 'numbered with the transgressors' in his death, it was in part because he had first numbered himself with those regarded as transgressors in his life. And he did it because it was what his Father was doing in the offer of his transforming presence to every man or woman who had ears to hear or eyes to see.

The picture of Jesus that I have offered is a subjective and a speculative one – like everybody else's. Its basic themes are ones that I believe are likely to go back to Jesus himself and not simply to have been imposed on him by later reflection. But it is also highly selective, highlighting aspects of the picture that seem particularly pertinent to a contemporary faith. Aspects of more immediate concern to the conditions of the first century have been played down. Other interpreters would certainly come up with pictures with a variety of different emphases. But with all those allowances made, it may still, I hope, give some impression of how the figure of Jesus, as the Gospels depict him, can contribute to our understanding of God and to our awareness of him as a transforming power in the world.

Interlude VI: Modern Study of the Gospels

The growth of scientific and historical study over the last two hundred years has led to a transformation of our understanding of the world and of past history. The Bible too has been the subject of intensive scholarly study during that same period. The impact of that study, generally spoken of as 'biblical criticism', has had a similar transforming effect on our understanding of the Bible. The cautious (some may have thought unduly sceptical) view of how much we can say historically about Jesus with any confidence that I put forward in the last chapter is, I believe, an inescapable consequence of such study. So it is worth saying a bit more about what biblical criticism involves when applied to the Gospels.

The word 'criticism' has strongly negative overtones; it suggests a deliberate intention to find fault, to look for mistakes. But that is not the basic meaning of the word. It means the process of forming a judgment – which is itself another word with some negative overtones, albeit not nearly such strong ones; it is common enough to speak of good or favourable judgments. The historical critic or the literary critic is not trying to find fault with history or literature; they are trying to work out what is involved in reaching good judgments about historical or literary matters. That is what Gospel criticism sets out to do. And since the Gospels are both records of the life of Jesus and also writings designed to inform and guide the life of the church of their day, Gospel criticism has much in common with the work of both historical and literary critics. So what forms does it take and what can it achieve?

Since the Gospels are texts, the first step is to be as sure as we can just what the text is. The earliest full manuscripts that we have are from the fourth to fifth centuries; most are considerably later, though some papyrus fragments from the third, or even the second century contain incomplete texts of some New Testament books. There are lots of mostly minor differences between these various surviving texts. As they were copied by hand, changes crept in from a very early stage. Sometimes the scribe just carelessly wrote the wrong letter or word, as we all do on occasion in similar circumstances. But on occasion the scribe found something in the text before him that didn't seem right to him, and 'corrected' it to make it read better. One example: early in Mark's Gospel, Jesus meets a leper and (so the Authorized Version has it) was 'moved with pity'; but the Revised English Bible says he 'was moved with anger'. The evidence of the manuscripts is divided. The latter, more surprising reading is almost certainly right. One can see why a scribe corrected it, but it is difficult to see how the variant arose if 'pity' was what the text had said in the first place. There are several places where it is not easy to decide what the original reading was. That can make a difference to the precise sense of the text, but such uncertainties are not in general serious enough or frequent enough to affect the overall meaning of the Gospels. By and large we are well served by our texts – though it does make quite a difference to the way one reads Mark if one accepts the scholarly consensus that the gospel originally ended at chapter 16 verse 8 without any account of a resurrection appearance, and that the final twelve verses printed in the Authorized Version are a later addition.

The historical reliability of the Gospels is another matter. Historians are, of course, used to probing behind written accounts and distinguishing between what is likely to go back to the earliest record and what is a later modification. It is what they do all the time. But there are features of the Gospel accounts that make them particularly difficult to handle. There are virtually no other sources with which to compare and check them – enough to discount the suggestion sometimes made that the Gospels are pure fiction with no foundation at all in actual history, but not enough to take us much further. Moreover the Gospels have a high ratio of miracle stories. Again there is nothing very surprising in that; so do a good many historical records from ancient times. But though such stories often help to illuminate the attitudes and expectations of people in the period in question, the historian regularly discounts their literal truth. And that is no arbitrary prejudice; it is a proper and necessary assumption of the historian's detective work in probing back behind the written record.

The Gospel records are, of course, not a single account, although they now appear within the covers of a single book. They are four separate accounts, though it is clear that both Matthew and Luke made use of Mark's Gospel. That is both a further problem and a help in our quest; a further problem because it shows how ready the evangelists were to change the information they had, even without other evidence to warrant such changes; a help because it enables us to see them at work and so to understand better what they were up to. Again an example will help: in Mark's account, the rich young ruler greets Jesus with the words, 'Good Teacher, what must I do to win eternal life?', to which Jesus replies 'Why do you call me good? No one is good except God alone'; Matthew's version of the interchange reads differently, with the rich young ruler saying 'Teacher, what good must I do to attain eternal life?' and Jesus replying 'Good? why do you ask me about that? One alone is good.' Matthew, it would seem, was unwilling to include a story in which Jesus differentiates himself so firmly from the unique goodness of God, and has rewritten the story to avoid that implication. That gives us an insight into the way Matthew thought and the way he composed his Gospel.

Clues of this kind help the historian in his or her work. So does a steadily increasing knowledge of Jewish history, life and customs of the time. But there is no escaping the fact that the process, however unavoidable and however responsibly done, remains a speculative one and its outcome always far from certain. Leaving on one side the sensational fringe whose writings tend to receive an unjustifiable share of coverage in the press, the variety of scholarly conclusions is still striking, not only on matters of detail but even in their fundamental portraiture of Jesus. Some see him as standing in the tradition of Jewish holy men of the time; others as an apocalyptic prophet expecting the end of the world in the near future; others as one who made firm, if veiled messianic claims on his own behalf; others again see him as primarily a moral teacher; and yet others as a champion and agitator on behalf of the poor. Those varied assessments are by no means all mutually exclusive, but the differences of emphasis make for significantly different understandings of Jesus. We may judge some more well-grounded than others, but there is little prospect of our achieving a more assured account of the original message and ministry of Jesus that will command general agreement. On these historical issues reasoned judgments are certainly possible, but they are bound to remain provisional and open to revision.

Literary critics concentrate on the overall nature of a work, what the author is trying to achieve and how the text holds together and makes its impact on the reader. If we think of the different Gospels simply as resource material for trying to construct a single, reliable account of Jesus as he was, we are sure to miss much of the distinctive message that each evangelist was setting out to convey. But there is an overlap between the attempt to understand the particular emphasis of each Gospel writer and the kind of enquiry pursued by the historian. Matthew's alteration of Mark's text, as in the example we have just looked at, tells us more about Matthew's outlook than about the actual words of Jesus. We may be unable to get back to the latter with any confidence, but the change Matthew has made throws light on how he is seeking to present the figure of Jesus. Furthermore you can't grasp an ancient author's aims very well without some knowledge of the culture and the literary conventions of the time. Some literary critics play down the importance of this attempt to enter into the author's mind. That, like the historical enquiry, seems to them too speculative an undertaking to yield fruitful results. They prefer to concentrate simply on the text that we have and ask how it functions in practice, without reference to the author's original intentions. That approach too can help, though I am not myself very convinced of its worth if it really eschews interest in the author's intentions altogether.

So all such forms of 'criticism' are simply more expert attempts to do the sorts of thing that every reader of the Gospels already tries to do in a more amateur way. But the critic can't do the whole job for us. Every act of reading and understanding a written text involves a process of assimilation into the reader's own already existing view of things. That view may be altered by the reading of the text, but it also contributes to the way we understand what we read. At first hearing that may sound like a disadvantage, but it isn't really. All understanding of the past, even that of the purest antiquarian, cannot help but be in some measure an understanding from the viewpoint of his or her own time. And for the Christian reader of the Scriptures this feature of understanding, which critical study brings out so strongly, is an encouraging reminder of how our reading of scriptural texts from the past can contribute to a life-long process of growth in Christian faith and understanding in the present.

7

Spirit

*Can we claim to have experience
of God?*

I turn now to the second, more general implication of the
notion of God's incarnation in the human person of Jesus
that I proposed earlier. There I suggested that the doctrine
of the incarnation 'symbolizes the intimacy of God's involvement with the world'. And in the last chapter I also suggested
that something very similar is a central theme running
through the parables of Jesus: if our eyes are open to see the
deeper significance of what is happening around us, they will
lead us to recognize there the transforming presence of God.

But what does such talk really mean? I have already
acknowledged that the idea that God is in providential control
of how the historical events that so vitally affect our lives
turn out, or of how our own individual lives meet with good
fortune or disaster, in the sort of way the biblical story seems
to assume, simply cannot be sustained. It ill accords both
with our scientific knowledge and with a belief in God's moral
character. Doesn't it follow, then, that any talk of God's
intimate involvement with the world will prove even harder
to understand or to accept? To understand – yes; to accept
– not necessarily. The concepts of Newtonian physics, for
example, are a good deal easier to understand than the concept of relativity to which they have had to yield place; but
that doesn't mean that the latter is not a truer account of
how the world is. What I want to suggest in this case is
that, even though it may seem most natural to think of the
relationship of God to the world to which faith points as a

straightforwardly causal one, parallel to the causal relation-
ships that the scientist studies, that is a mistake. It is a fundamentally different kind of relationship.

How then can we describe it? Is it possible for our minds
to get any intelligible grasp on it? I have already acknowledged that any such grasp is bound to be extremely limited.
Since it is *God's* relation to the world that we are trying to
understand, such understanding can only be of a very indirect
and symbolic kind. Perhaps the most appropriate language is
the language of 'presence'. Such language has strong roots in
the biblical tradition. The Psalmist speaks movingly of the
inescapability of God's presence:

> Whither shall I go then from thy spirit: or whither shall I
> go then from thy presence?
> If I climb up into heaven, thou art there: if I go down
> to hell, thou art there also.
> If I take the wings of the morning and remain in the
> uttermost parts of the sea,
> Even there also shall thy hand lead me, and thy right
> hand uphold me.

And the final words of the risen Christ in Matthew's Gospel
are the reassuring promise to the disciples of his presence:

> Lo, I am with you always, even unto the end of the world.

Presence, admittedly, sounds on first hearing a rather tame
and passive notion. But it often carries a much stronger and
more positive connotation. As every lover knows and as every
pastor knows, the presence of 'the other', or simply the presence of 'an other', can make all the difference to a situation;
it can turn a sense of emptiness into ecstasy or an unendurable
loss into a bearable sorrow. Presence can act as a powerful
agent of transformation.

The way in which Christians have traditionally spoken of
God, when thinking of God's relation to the world as a

powerfully transformative presence, is in terms of 'spirit'. The Hebrew word translated as 'spirit' in the Old Testament originally means 'breath' – that which makes the mysterious difference between a corpse and a living human being. Nowadays if we speak of the human spirit, the phrase is more likely to convey a moral or evaluative sense – not that which makes possible the bare fact of life as such, but rather that which enables a person to be what he or she ideally has it in him or her to become; a person of 'spirit' implies not just someone who is alive, but someone who is lively. The same word also meant 'wind', with the wind seen as a powerful, unpredictable source of energy.

All those shades of meaning contribute to the way in which the designation 'spirit' can enrich our understanding of God. To speak of God as 'spirit' is to affirm that it is because of God that the world is the living organism we know it to be, with its potential for the emergence and development of life. It also implies that it is because of God that human life has the potential to realize those personal qualities that we instinctively value and admire when we meet them. God is to be known not only in the unchanging aspects of our world, but in the dynamic of change also.

The underlying conviction that characterizes a strong sense of God's presence is the same as that which underlies belief in God as creator. That conviction, I argued earlier, is a response to the sense of wonder that there should be anything at all, especially anything with the strange emergent properties of human consciousness, goodness and love. Both forms of belief (God as creator and God as spirit) are, of course, symbols – pictures pointing to a truth that lies beyond the range of clear or precise definition. The language of creator is a more personal, but more distant and external image; the language of spirit suggests a less personal but more intimate presence. The two serve to complement one another.

In our reflections so far the more external images of Father and Son have been paramount. But commitment to the Christian way seldom derives simply from reflection on the fact of creation and the records of Jesus' life, death and resurrection. The more inward, experiential aspect of faith implicit in the designation of God as 'spirit' has normally a crucial role to play in the emergence of Christian conviction. But the 'experiential aspect of faith' is a difficult notion. What does it mean to speak of 'experience of God'?

In 1902 William James, the brother of Henry James and one of the leading psychologists of his day, published a famous book entitled *The Varieties of Religious Experience*. That book has done a lot to make the idea of religious experience or experience of God a familiar one in the twentieth century. But it has also done a lot to show how questionable a notion it is. For it showed not only how varied are the forms of experience that lay claim to being experiences of God, but also how bizarre their content often is. They may take the form of visions, or voices, or simply the still small voice of inner conviction. But despite the psychological immediacy and the undeniable authenticity with which they are experienced by those who have had them, they are so varied and the messages they are understood to convey so mutually inconsistent that they cannot all be accepted as true and reliable revelations of God. And in that case can any of them be so accepted?

I do not believe that they can – at least in the direct, unmediated and therefore unquestionable character that is frequently claimed for them. Just as words of Scripture are never direct words of God, but are also human words of the person who wrote them, so the form of any experience of God is necessarily affected by the social, cultural and religious context through which it is mediated. It is no coincidence that Buddhists tend to have visions of the Buddha, Catholics of the Virgin Mary and Protestants of the risen Christ. There is no by-passing the fallible, human process of interpretation that is involved in the shaping and the telling of all our experiences, including those that we think it right to describe as experiences of God. But that doesn't invalidate the possibility that such experiences may indeed be genuine pointers towards a presence of God in our world and to our consciousness. All that it rules out is the idea that the experiential aspect of faith can be a purely private matter, independent of the wider context in which our lives are set. None of our experiences, however deeply personal, is unaffected by the ideas and the people that surround us and that play so large a role in our development as unique human beings.

So the experiential aspect of faith that contributes to Christian conviction is likely to be linked in some way to the life of a Christian community. For it is the church which has preserved, practised and proclaimed Christian faith down the centuries; and it is through the continuing life of the church (in one of its many varied forms) that people are most likely to gain not merely some knowledge about Christianity (which books too can convey), but also some impression of what it might mean as a way of life to be followed. And that fits also with the fact that in the New Testament the primary emphasis in what is said about the gift of the Spirit is that it is given to the church. But before we take up questions relating to the church, there is another issue, arising even more directly out of this chapter, to be dealt with first.

8

The Trinity

Does it make sense to speak of
three persons and one God?

In earlier chapters I have written about the designations of
God as Father, Son and Spirit, presenting them as different
images, each of which helps us to envisage some fundamental
aspect of God's relation to us and to our world. However,
for Christian faith those names are much more than just
alternative designations for God. As 'Father, Son and Holy
Spirit' they come together to form the distinctive Christian
name for God. The doctrine of the Trinity, with its affirmation
of them as three persons but one God, is widely perceived as
the central and most all-embracing of Christian doctrines;
but it is also widely perceived as the most problematic and
paradoxical of doctrines. Does it make sense to speak of three
persons constituting one (personal) God? At times in the past
the mathematical paradoxicality of the doctrine has even been
treated as if it enhanced its religious value ('Firmly I believe
and truly / God is three and God is one'). What are we to
make of it? Tackling that question calls for a brief review of
how the doctrine arose.

It is generally recognized that the doctrine of the Trinity
as it has come to be believed in the church since the late
fourth century is not to be found in the Bible. There is nothing
surprising in that. All Christian doctrines go well beyond
what is directly stated or unquestionably implied by the biblical text. What we do find in the New Testament are a number
of places where affirmations about God are couched in a
triadic form. The two most famous examples are the parting

injunction of the risen Christ to the disciples at the end of Matthew's Gospel ('Go . . . and teach all nations, baptizing them in the name of the Father and of the Son and of the Holy Spirit') and the final blessing with which Paul closes his second letter to the Corinthians ('The grace of the Lord Jesus Christ, the love of God and the communion of the Holy Spirit be with you all'). But how are such formulae to be understood? They are not identical. Do they, indeed, imply the threefold nature of the one God (as the doctrine of the Trinity explicitly does) when in one case the designation 'God' names just one member of the three? Moreover there are plenty of twofold formulae that include no mention of the Spirit. For pagans, says Paul, there are many so-called gods, but 'for us there is but one God the Father from whom are all things . . . and one Lord Jesus Christ by whom are all things'. And there are some surprising threefold forms: the author of the first letter to Timothy (almost certainly not Paul himself) solemnly charges his reader 'before God and the Lord Jesus Christ and the elect angels'. And then there are still other apparently divine entities, such as the Word, who figures so prominently in the familiar opening of John's Gospel ('In the beginning was the Word and the Word was with God and the Word was God'). In many ways the Word seems very close in conception to the Spirit, but since the Word is made flesh as Jesus Christ there is a strong case for identifying the Word with the Son. All in all, the ways of speaking about God are much too variegated to fall into any single pattern. Threefold forms may figure most frequently, but even they are far from uniform. Moreover, while the doctrine of the Trinity asserts the equality of the three persons, in the New Testament the Father always appears to be 'greater' than the Son, sending the Son into the world, a Son who is regularly described as 'obedient' to his Father.

As the church grew in numbers and in geographical extent, and consequently developed more organized institutional structures as well, this issue cried out for further clarification: what were the implications of Christ's coming and of the emergence of the church for the understanding of God that Christians had inherited along with the Old Testament scriptures? It was a natural enough urge arising out of the church's internal life of teaching and worship, but one that was further reinforced by pagan taunts that Christians worshipped a human God who had been born quite recently and had died a criminal's death.

The debates that followed were long and complex, fuelled by deep devotion and profound thought, but also by personal rivalries and ecclesiastical power politics. Two principles resisted all attempts to override them and combined to determine the outcome. First, the three divine names, Father, Son and Holy Spirit, it was felt, could not just be alternative names for the same reality. Their respective roles in the story of Christ's life, death and resurrection, and also in the continuing story of the church's life and worship, required that they must be in some sense distinct realities. But secondly there could not be more than one God, nor could there be differing degrees of Godhead: either of those solutions to the problem would constitute a relapse into the errors of polytheism to which the church was implacably opposed. So each of the three must be fully God, in the only proper meaning of that word. The outcome was to affirm that God was one, but that within that unity there was a threefold distinction (in reality, not just in name) between the co-equal Father, Son and Holy Spirit. If it surpassed human powers to conceive or imagine how such a tri-unity could be, that was only to be expected in relation to the mysterious nature of God's being; and the evidence of both Scripture and experience showed that it must be so. Indeed, it was hard to know what term to use to refer to these distinguishable, but not separate, entities within the one Godhead. Augustine justified his use of the Latin word *persona* by saying that, inadequate though it was, the only alternative would be silence. But the use of its English equivalent, 'person', has proved seriously misleading. For it was certainly never intended to convey the full sense in which we now use the word 'person' to refer to an individual human being.

Until quite recently many theologians have tended to play down the natural implication of the word 'person' and to suggest that it might be better to speak of three different 'modes of being'. At the moment there is a swing back to a greater stress on the distinct personal identity of each of the three. That, it is suggested, offers a valuable reminder that the divinely given ideal for the lives of men and women, 'made in God's image', is one of finding the meaning of our existence, not as isolated individuals but in the richness of our relationship with others. God is a social as truly as an individual reality – and so are we.

My own reaction to this continuing debate is to re-emphasize the symbolic nature of the language on which all such reflections are based. No one symbol is ever sufficient to provide firm or safe guidance to the understanding of God. But the threefold symbolism of Father, Son and Spirit, which underlies all ideas of the Trinity, does, I have tried to show, offer invaluable guidelines to Christian thought about the nature and purposes of God. Father, Son and Holy Spirit name three different ways in which God is most directly accessible to us: in the mysterious existence of anything at all; in the transformative power of the historical figure of Jesus; and in the inwardness of profound human, and particularly Christian experience – or, to put it in more traditional language, as creator, redeemer and sanctifier. But none of these ways operates in independence of the other. And all this finds succinct and powerful expression in the doctrine of the Trinity. But to go on and insist that that doctrine warrants affirmations about a threefoldness that is characteristic of the very being of God as such seems to involve using that symbolism in ways that are inappropriate to its nature. It is not the sort of knowledge to which it is possible for us to aspire. We can quite properly allow trinitarian thought to inform our ideas about God and our worship of God, without worrying about whether, by doing so, we may be committing ourselves to self-contradictory beliefs about God – indeed we would be sadly impoverished if we did not use it in that fundamental way. There are many grave problems about how we are to understand the mystery of God's being, but the problem of how God can be both three and one is not at the heart of the matter.

Interlude VII: The Development of Doctrine

The doctrine of the Trinity is only one example of a doctrine with roots in the New Testament that grew into something of a very different kind from its beginnings. Most doctrines have a similar history. So it is worth asking how we should view the relation between these more developed doctrines and the original teaching of Jesus and the apostles.

One way in which it has often been put is to say that later doctrines are simply making explicit what was always implicit in the earlier teaching. That can be understood in a stricter or a looser sense. The stricter view sees the later teaching as drawing out the logical implications of what had been earlier taught, in the way that the conclusion of a deductive argument is already implicit in the premises from which it is drawn, even though one may have been unaware of it until the inference is consciously made. Thus the formal doctrine about the person of Christ, agreed at the Council of Chalcedon in AD 451, which affirms that he had both a fully divine and a fully human nature, is sometimes said to be logically implied by the varied ways in which the New Testament speaks about him as both a divine figure and as a suffering human being. The looser view uses a biological rather than a logical analogy. The earlier teaching is then seen as a seed which, though it does not contain the subsequent doctrine already latent within itself, does lead on to it as naturally as an acorn grows into an oak.

This second account seems clearly preferable; it depicts better the gradual historical change from the earlier to the later stages in the development of a doctrine, and is also more appropriate to the symbolic character of all religious imagery, which does not fit well with the idea of logical deduction. In this form the notion is certainly an attractive one. It seems to be able to do justice to the radical difference of kind between earlier and later forms of Christian teaching while still holding on to the idea of an unchanging core of truth underlying the whole process.

Nevertheless it has two serious difficulties, of a kind that has already emerged in the course of our reflections. In the first place the whole picture assumes that, however much development may be required, we have in the Bible or in the original teaching of Jesus or in the preaching of the apostles a firm nugget of unqualified truth on which Christian doctrines can be based. But, as we have seen, the nature of the Bible and of our evidence about the teaching of Jesus and the apostles is of a kind that simply rules out the possibility of such a starting point. And secondly, re-expressing old beliefs in a new cultural setting can never be a matter of translating old ideas into a new language with no change of substance at all. A change of culture involves a new way not just of stating things but also of how we see things. A new cultural context affects not only how we express old beliefs, but in some measure the content of what we believe as well.

These criticisms of the notion of a core of unchanging truth that runs through all the changing forms of Christian doctrine find plenty of support in Christian history. The expression of beliefs in a new social or intellectual setting has seldom avoided being influenced to some degree by the society and the intellectual spirit of the age to which it belongs. Even the more conservative statements of Christian doctrine today usually involve some repudiation, conscious or unconscious, of once firmly held doctrines. Thus the traditional doctrine that Christ had a fully divine nature was normally understood in the past to imply that he had the divine attribute of omniscience. Today even the most vigorous upholders of the doctrine defined at the Council of Chalcedon are likely to disclaim any such belief. And the reason for that disclaimer is the greatly enhanced understanding now available to us of how fundamentally all human character and all human knowledge are affected by the particular historical conditions of our birth and our environment.

To ascribe omniscience to one whom we also affirm to be fully human appears to most people today to be not merely an astounding claim, as it always did, but an incomprehensible one.

If this analysis of how doctrines develop is along the right lines, it has important repercussions on what is an appropriate attitude to adopt towards earlier formulations of Christian belief and also towards Christian belief today. The writers of the scriptural books, the apostles in their preaching and the bishops who drew up the early creeds were all involved in the same struggle – trying to find appropriate language to communicate what they had learnt and experienced of God to the particular audience to whom they were addressing themselves through the written or the spoken word. There is no reason to believe that what they came up with was ever perfectly satisfactory even in their own time; it certainly cannot be expected to apply perfectly in ours. So giving expression to Christian belief is never a matter of simply being faithful to the teachings of the past, of preserving the deposit of truth as it has been handed on to us by previous generations. Every generation has the task of constructing forms of belief and practice appropriate to its own times and culture. We won't always get it right – nor can we judge with confidence how far we may have succeeded or where our failures lie. But the greatest failure of all is to fail to see that the task is a creative one, where the only way to proceed is by trial and error, by a process of shared experience and shared debate between Christians. All statements of doctrine are necessarily provisional – however unchanging the truth about God that they are attempting to express.

9

Salvation

What does it mean to be saved?

A good deal of what I have written so far has dealt with what Christians believe about God, coming to its climax with the doctrine of the Trinity in the last chapter. This reflects an emphasis that the church has placed, right through Christian history, on the importance of holding right beliefs. But it would be seriously misleading if that were to give the impression that a proper understanding of the nature of God was in itself the essential goal of Christian faith. Where right belief about God has been stressed, it has been because that was seen as necessary to receiving the salvation that God offers to the world through 'our *Saviour* Jesus Christ'. It is first and foremost as a way of salvation that Christianity has presented itself.

However, for people today the language of 'salvation', the whole idea that men and women need to be 'saved', has far less resonance than it did in the past. Many tend to associate such words with what they regard as peripheral manifestations of Christianity, such as the Salvation Army or the preaching of extreme evangelical sects. But we cannot simply set the whole idea of salvation to one side as easily as that. Its role in the origins and in the continuing story of Christianity is far too central for us to dismiss it so lightly. So how is such language to be understood?

In the Old Testament it is in the form of hope for the liberation of Israel from captivity or oppression by one of the stronger, surrounding powers that the hope of salvation most frequently finds expression. But we meet also with more comprehensive forms of hope for a transformed earth, where swords are beaten into ploughshares and the lion lies down with the lamb. In the New Testament we find similar hopes expressed for the completion of the work that God has begun with Jesus's proclamation of the coming of God's kingdom, his resurrection from the dead and the emergence of the church. At times those hopes are restricted to Christian believers, with all who do not share that belief condemned to punishment and destruction. At other times they take on a more comprehensive form with the expectation of a new heaven and a new earth, a time when God will be all in all. Similar aspirations have been a continuing feature of the life of the church throughout its history, sometimes indeed in bizarre and literal forms. But essentially they need to be seen as what they have always been: hopes that defy spelling out in intelligible terms, but are the stuff of visions ('new Jerusalem coming down . . . out of heaven like a bride adorned for her husband') or of prayer ('thy will be done on earth as it is in heaven'). They are not to be treated as specific predictions of the future, but rather as deep-seated human hopes finding expression in forms shaped by the Christian story and by the faith in God that stems from it.

All such dreams heighten our sense of the radical difference between the world as it is and the world as it ought to be. They can function (as Marxist critics have insisted) as an opiate to the people, a substitute fulfilment which discourages commitment to the struggle against present wrong. Or they can function (as Martin Luther King's famous speech suggests) as an encouragement and inspiration to such commitment.

But however that particular dispute be resolved, for most people such hopes are likely to prove too vast, too distant and too tenuous to relate at all closely to their daily lives. So it is hardly surprising that it is in more individual terms that the idea of salvation has had its greatest impact. There is no direct conflict between the two; the idea of individual salvation is not an alternative to the wider vision, but an essential part of it. Any transformation of the comprehensive kind implicit in the wider vision must involve a radical transformation of the individual lives that make up our human world. That human lives are in need of such transformation is hardly open to question. The traditional Christian language about 'sin' finds ample justification in the ruthlessness and greed, both individual and corporate, whose effects are only too evident in the contemporary world. The forms of transformation needed are varied and find expression in the great range of imagery associated with the idea of salvation. Embittered conflicts, domestic, social and ethnic, cry out for a spirit of forgiveness and reconciliation; private addictions and social oppression exercise a tyranny over human lives, which long for liberation and freedom; the entail of the past often leads to a sense of hopelessness and despair, from which there seems to be no escape, no way of beginning again. It is these needs that are addressed by the Christian message of salvation as a way of forgiveness, liberation and new birth.

These are powerful images, but like all imagery they are not without their dangers. They suggest a once-for-all change, in which the effect is instantaneous and our role is purely passive. The offender is forgiven; the prisoner is set free; the child is born. The story of Paul's apparently instantaneous conversion on the Damascus road from passionate persecutor of the church to its intrepid and powerful propagator is the most famous example of such a transformation. But however abrupt the change may have been on that occasion, it is a mistake to treat it as a paradigm case to which all experiences of salvation should conform. The transformation of human life that we look for takes time, and other aspects of Christian teaching give that fact full recognition. To take the imagery too literally and conclude that salvation ought always to be of that all-or-nothing character is likely to mess up not only our understanding of salvation but also the lives that are affected by such an understanding.

So how should the language of Christian salvation be understood? Its positive implications can be spelt out in three ways:

1. Human lives can be radically changed. For all the immense influence of our genes and of our upbringing on the kind of persons that we are and have it in us to become, we are not simply trapped for ever, unable to modify the inheritance we have received.

2. It is crucial to such transformation that we should not remain locked up in ourselves but be open to the Spirit, to the presence of God mediated to us through the church and through other human lives.

3. The story of Christ's life, death and resurrection depicts the way the presence of God can work in human life, and provides the conditions that make that power accessible to us. Traditional faith speaks of him as the one who bears the punishment and wins our forgiveness; the one who conquers the forces of evil and sets us, their prisoners, free; the one who dies that we may live. These, as we have already noted, are powerful images, but ones that are easily open to misunderstanding. Taken literally, the first, for example, implies an unacceptable notion of God as one who requires punishment of someone, innocent or guilty, before forgiveness is forthcoming. But taken symbolically, they are all vivid ways of depicting how the story of Christ's death and the notion of God that it embodies can transform human attitudes and human lives.

So salvation is concerned with the transformation of human life. Barriers to human flourishing are broken down; growth in the life of the spirit is made possible through openness to the Spirit of God. All this is meant to be a part of our experience now, however far short of the ideal its actual realization may prove to be. But it is not regarded as something that is limited to the span of our life on earth. Being in its essence a relationship with God, it is seen as something that cannot be broken by death. What we are to make of that final aspect of salvation must await our final chapter.

10

Other Faiths

*If Christianity is true, are all other
religions false?*

The church down the ages has not only taught that belief in
Christ is a way of salvation, but has also insisted that it is
the only way of salvation. That judgment carried with it a
strongly negative attitude to other religions which also
claimed to offer a way of salvation to their followers. Nor
was that assessment of other forms of religious faith often
felt to be problematic. But those days are long past. We live
in a pluralist society. No longer can the adherents of other
faiths be dismissed as benighted heathen from distant lands.
They include friends and neighbours, some of whom put
many Christians to shame by the depth of their spirituality
and the quality of their lives. So today some old questions
press themselves on us with a new intensity. Is the belief that
Christianity has an exclusive hold on religious truth and on
the way of salvation an integral part of the Christian gospel?
And if it is, is such a belief tenable? What status are we to
ascribe to the other great religions of the world? Are they no
more than the delusions or demonic perversions of the truth
that Christians have frequently alleged them to be in the past?
   The dilemma is a real one. Judaism, Islam, Hinduism and
Buddhism are vastly different from Christianity and from one
another, and we should not play down the extent of those
differences in belief and practice. So if we acknowledge some
measure of truth in religions other than our own, does that
not imply a weakening in the strength of our commitment to
our own faith? Or is the more positive attitude to them, which

seems to so many people today to be appropriate, compatible with allegiance to Christianity as a true way of faith and practice?

Some Christians recoil from any such suggestion as clearly unfaithful to the Christian gospel. Is it not ruled out from the start, they argue, by sayings of Jesus such as: 'I am the way, the truth and the life; no one comes to the Father but by me'? It is not hard to find sayings of that nature in the Bible, and they have had considerable influence on subsequent thought and practice. But we have already seen that texts and teachings of the Bible, including sayings attributed to Jesus, cannot properly be taken over in that direct sort of way. We need to look at the issue in a broader perspective. The lines along which I propose to deal with it here are already implicit in much that has been said earlier in the course of our discussion.

Christianity has roots in a religious sense of awe and wonder that seems to be a fundamental aspect of almost all human experience. But its articulation as a specific form of faith has grown up over many centuries by way of a particular historical development and a distinctive cultural tradition. Out of that history, particular events, stories and images have come to shape the ideas and the rituals by which men and women have sought to direct their lives. Those deeply rooted ideas and images were moulded into their distinctively Christian form through the life, death and resurrection of Jesus and all that sprang from them. So the specific way in which Christianity points to the divine mystery and establishes the form of a characteristically Christian relationship with God is the fruit of the contingent historical tradition that led up to Jesus and continued on into the life of the church. As I have already argued, the fact that it developed in that way, one profoundly influenced by its particular historical context, does not prevent its being the vehicle for genuine apprehension of and relationship with God; but it does mean that such apprehension of God by Christian believers is bound to be both partial and provisional, open always to enlargement, correction and revision.

If that is anything like a valid account of how religious traditions develop, it must apply to other religions as well as to Christianity. They have had different founding events and have grown up in different cultural settings with different stories and images, through which they have sought to interpret and relate to the ultimate mystery. It is perfectly possible that, through the different interpretative prisms of their dominant images and motifs, they also (or at least some of them) may embody valid apprehensions of the divine, despite the extent of their differences from Christianity and from one another.

The qualification in brackets is important. The case that I am putting forward does not imply that everything that lays claim to the name of 'religion' merits the kind of positive assessment that I am suggesting. There are forms of religious faith and practice that need to be challenged as foolish or evil, and sometimes both. But that there are faiths other than Christianity which demand our respect for their deep insights into the mystery of human life and for the profound spirituality that they nurture is now widely acknowledged. In recent years, for example, the Roman Catholic Church has come to teach not simply that adherents of other religions may find salvation, but that when they do so they are to be understood as finding it through the structures of the religion to which they belong, and not in spite of them. It does not follow from this that all such religions are of equal truth or worth. What does follow is that the fundamental fault line between truth and falsity in religious belief and practice is not one that lies straightforwardly between Christianity and all other religions. It is one that exists within every religion, including Christianity.

Some of these religions, like Christianity, incorporate in their traditional teaching claims about the absolute and irreformable nature of the truths that they hold. But if my general analysis is correct, those claims have no more justification in their case than in the case of Christianity. In every case they are to be seen as dangerous displacements of the absoluteness that properly belongs to the goal of the religious quest on to the always partial and provisional sets of beliefs through which the particular religions seek to articulate their goal.

This is a book about problems inherent in Christian faith. So there is no need to pursue this complex question much further. What I am suggesting does not imply that we should be looking for some common denominator which would serve as a universal form of faith; it implies rather that we should embark on a process of mutual exploration and learning between religions. That road will certainly be long and difficult. Christian history shows how difficult (and still far from complete) has been the process of differing Christian perspectives learning to move away from attitudes of mutual recrimination and denunciation to ones of mutual respect, cooperation and learning. The similar process between different religions will no doubt prove even more complex and hazardous. But if the possibility of such a process exists, then there is no need to regard Christianity as caught on the horns of an insoluble dilemma – bound to relinquish either its own claim to religious truth or else any acknowledgment that other religious traditions may also be giving expression to genuine forms of religious belief.

What then of the missionary dimension that is so marked a feature of Christian practice? It is not ruled out, but it is not left unaffected either. If Christianity has proved to be a distinctive and life-enhancing truth for us, then it is right that we should seek to share it with others. But it is not right that we should act as if it was *the* truth to the exclusion of all other forms of religious allegiance. The goal of such sharing need not always be one of conversion, whereby others abandon their existing form of religious allegiance and identify themselves with ours. Sometimes that may prove the appropriate outcome. But in other cases it may be rather the incorporation of new and enriching insights into an existing form of faith. And that can be a mutual experience. Christians too may look for correction and enlargement of their faith through what they learn from those with whom they seek to share their own. It is not without significance that among those who have contributed to the way of thinking outlined in this chapter are to be found Christian missionaries. Some of those who have gone to live and work as missionaries in countries where some other faith has been dominant have, through personal friendships and through close and sensitive study of that other faith, developed a profound respect for its teaching and its spirituality – while remaining firmly committed to their own Christian faith. They have not ceased to be missionaries, but have been missionaries of a different style and spirit.

11

The Public Face of the Church

Witness for the prosecution or for the defence?

I have spoken of the church as the place where it is possible to acquire 'an impression of what Christianity might mean as a way of life to be followed', and suggested that for many it has been the cradle in which Christian commitment has been born and nurtured. True as that may be, there are also many for whom the life of the church serves not as an encouragement to adopt the claims and practices of Christian faith but as a major dissuasive to the acceptance of its claims and the adoption of its ways. It does not need much reflection on the church's historical record to remind us how ambivalent its witness has been.

The blood of the martyrs, the saying goes, was the seed of the church. The fortitude and conviction with which many early Christians faced torture and death rather than renounce their faith was undoubtedly one factor in the remarkable progress whereby the church moved from being a despised cult at the margin of the Roman world to become the established religion of the empire. But the history of the church figures Christians not only in the role of martyrs but also in that of the makers of martyrs. The story of the Inquisition, for example, reveals the systematic use of torture and death for those who would not conform to the orthodox faith. Sometimes the same person figures as both victim and perpetrator of martyrdom. Archbishop Cranmer, for example, who was burnt at the stake by catholic Christians, officially for erroneous teaching about the nature of Christ's presence in the eucharistic elements, had himself been responsible for condemning to death some who held more extreme Protestant views than his own on that same issue.

A similar admixture of good and evil is to be seen in many other aspects of the church's life. Three further examples will suffice. In the development of human knowledge, the Christian belief that the world is the handiwork of the one creator God did much to help establish a framework of thought that provided fertile soil for the growth of modern science; it encouraged the expectation that the world would prove to be an ordered and unitive whole, whose workings were accessible to the human mind with its affinity to the mind of God in whose image men and women had been created. Yet time and again, when aspects of that new knowledge appeared to conflict with beliefs that the church ascribed to divine revelation, it fought hard to suppress them, as the familiar stories of Galileo and Darwin remind us. Again, in the never-ending struggle of human freedom against oppression, Christianity has fuelled both the coercion of the oppressor and the resistance of the oppressed. In South America in recent decades priests of the Roman Catholic Church have provided justification and support for dictatorial regimes, at the same time that other priests of the same communion have been a source of inspiration and strength to their downtrodden subjects. Finally the missionary history of the church wears a similar Janus-like complexion. It contains records of great personal sacrifice and compassionate service on the part of countless missionaries. But such records go hand in hand with accounts of gross arrogance and harshly destructive insensitivity towards cultures other than their own.

This Jekyll and Hyde-like character has been a mark of the church from its first days right up to the present. Writing to the Corinthian church Paul speaks of it as the body of Christ and as the bride of Christ, while in the same breath castigating it for its divisive quarrels, its social snobbery and its gross immorality. And even as I write the church is having formally to apologize for its failure to speak out or act on behalf of Jews at the time of the Holocaust, and for its failure to acknowledge or take action about priests guilty of the abuse of children. Were it not for fear that the language might seem to trivialize the matter, it would be tempting to sum up by applying to the church the words used of the little girl with the curl in the middle of her forehead: 'when she was good, she was very, very good, but when she was bad she was horrid'.

If then the history of the church from beginning to end displays the same combination of good and evil that characterizes not only little girls but human society in general, what credibility can we give to its claim to be the place where the transforming power of God, made effective in the world through Christ, is primarily to be found?

The most striking feature of the bleak crimes that disfigure the record of the church's past is that they are not just examples of ordinary human failure to live up to one's ideals. That certainly is a part of the story, but it is not the most significant part. Many of the faults that we have been recalling arose directly out of positive aspects of Christian faith and not simply out of neglect of them. Anti-semitism, and other forms of spiritual arrogance or persecuting zeal, all grew out of the church's conviction that it had been given a unique grasp on revealed truth, which it must at all costs defend and propagate. That fact underscores the extent to which the sins of the church may be felt to undermine the credibility of its gospel. If it is the distinctively religious nature of its claims that gives rise to its persecuting zeal, is that not strong evidence that those claims should be rejected?

The objection is one that needs to be taken seriously. What can be said by way of reply? In the first place, the history of the twentieth century lends little support to the suggestion that casting out the demon of Christianity would provide a cure from the human propensity for persecuting zeal. The recent records of Nazism and Stalinism show that non-religious ideologies can fuel every bit as evil an abuse of power as religious ones. The evils of the church's history may be valid grounds for rejecting many of the church's claims on its own behalf. They are not so clearly valid grounds for rejecting its religious message altogether.

However else one may choose to describe the church, it is an institution with rules and authority structures like other institutions. That brings both gain and loss. It provides the stability that is needed for human growth and flourishing, and above all a setting within which the gospel can be handed on to future generations. But the rules and structures that are needed to give shape to corporate life can also prove repressive and restrictive of proper freedom. And that has certainly been as true of the church as it has been of political institutions.

No institution is wholly free of evil effects. Some of those evils arise almost inescapably from the way in which the good and evil consequences of institutional life are so intimately bound up together. Rules that are necessary to safeguard the well-being of the vulnerable cannot always avoid curbing the freedom of others. But much of it is the fruit of the corruption that so easily accompanies the exercise of power and the opportunity of amassing wealth – and there has been plenty of that within the church.

Furthermore, there is truth in the old Latin tag *corruptio optimi pessima* – the worst form of corruption is corruption of the good. Pure, unadulterated evil is generally lacking in staying power; it has an inherent tendency towards self-destruction. The perversion of the good is often more dangerous; the underlying good intention preserves, even in its perverted state, the ability to justify itself and so to press on with the abuses and the cruelties it has adopted in the pursuit of its goal. Many a protest campaign, like some forms of the contemporary Animal Liberation movement, has been led on in large measure by the nobility of its original ideal to commit crimes that are in sharp conflict with that originating spirit. That an underlying good can lend strength to the most abominable evil does not invalidate the goodness of that underlying good. It may even be a kind of inverted testimony to it. Its strength, even in an evil guise, bears witness to the importance of its role in human life. The argument is a dangerous one, and must not be pressed too far. It does nothing whatever to excuse the evils perpetrated by the church. But it may serve to show how it might be possible for such evils to be so integrally interwoven into the life of a body that is, nonetheless, also a special conveyor of religious truth and grace.

In the arguments that I have been putting forward already in this book, there has been a recurrent stress on one particular theme: the kind of certainty that the church has traditionally claimed to be the appropriate attitude with which the believer ought to embrace its teachings cannot be sustained. The indirectness of the language in which all religious beliefs are necessarily expressed and the nature of the Bible as the primary source of Christian revelation both militate strongly against any such claim. Yet it was precisely the claim to a certain and exclusive hold on truth that has been at the heart of the church's deep-set tendency to oppress those who rejected its teaching. But that, as I have been arguing throughout, is not the only way in which Christianity can be, or indeed has been held. There is a way of faith which is less self-confident about the manner in which it understands and affirms its Christian beliefs, but which is no less committed to Christianity as a way of believing and living. Holding the faith in such a way is not only more consistent with the evidence for religious faith that we have been surveying. It is likely also to prove less prone to the persecuting zeal that has so marred the history of the church.

Interlude VIII: From Jesus to the Church

The contrast between Jesus, the itinerant preacher with his disciples in Galilee, and the institutional church with its hierarchical structure of bishops, priests and deacons could hardly be greater. I have already argued that any movement, seeking continuity through future generations, is bound to develop some more settled organisation than was needed to get it going at the start. But it is worth pausing to reflect on how this particular transition took place.

At first the church expanded through the missionary activity of apostles like Paul and through the movement of ordinary Christians in the course of trade or other business. At that stage, as Paul's letters show, the founding father of a new congregation exercised great authority in directing its life, even though not being a resident member of it. But responsible local officers were clearly needed. In course of time their role grew in importance. There were no special church buildings, so the meeting-place for the community was usually the most commodious home available from among its members. It was natural enough for the head of that household often to become the head of the local church as well, carrying over into that office the very considerable authority that was traditionally accorded to the head of a Roman household. In the New Testament the Pastoral Epistles (that is, the two letters to Timothy and the one to Titus, which bear Paul's name but which were almost certainly written after Paul's death by someone anxious to ensure that Paul's legacy should be carried on effectively) spell out the solid, conservative qualities to be looked for in appointing such a leader.

These early Christian communities did not have an easy

time. Made up of men and women from varied social backgrounds and subject to sporadic persecution of an official, or more often unofficial kind, they were liable to dissensions from within and attacks from without. Jesus is recorded in Matthew's Gospel as teaching his followers to forgive those who do them wrong 'not seven times, but seventy times seven'. But was it possible to order the life of a community on that basis? Could members of the congregation who flagrantly abused the trust of others be forgiven every time? Were those who renounced their faith under the threat of persecution simply to be received back when the danger had passed? Problems of this kind called for strong, recognized leadership.

Early in the second century Ignatius, Bishop of Antioch, was, like Paul, taken to Rome to face martyrdom, and wrote letters to the churches in Asia Minor which he visited on his journey. In them he warns of the dangers arising from dissension and persecution, and, to safeguard against them, he insists on the need for absolute obedience to the bishop (or 'overseer' as the Greek word *episkopos* literally means) of the local community, together with the presbyters ('elders') and deacons ('assistants'). Obedience to the single bishop was a symbol of obedience to the one God.

So the precariousness of the early church's situation put a high premium on obedience to the bishop, and to the ministry more generally. But obedience to the bishop was not unqualified. What happened if different bishops taught different things? The bishop of Rome, the city which had seen the martyrdom of Peter and Paul as well as being the capital city of the Empire, always had a special prestige. But it was loyalty to one's own local tradition that was paramount. When later in the second century Rome and Ephesus quarrelled over the right date for the celebration of Easter (an issue that was still a serious bone of contention between Celtic and Roman Christians in the seventh century), the Bishop of Ephesus was adamant that loyalty to God required loyalty to the local tradition in which he and his community had been reared. Each bishop, it was widely accepted at the time, had complete authority in his own diocese. Divergence of belief and practice in the wider church might be regrettable, but no bishop owed obedience to any other bishop.

But what if a bishop turned out to be corrupt, to have been guilty of offering sacrifice rather than face martyrdom in time of persecution, or to teach things that seemed to others to be not merely different but in flagrant contradiction of the gospel message? In such cases obedience was not appropriate, but who was to judge when such a pass had been reached? There were courts of appeal to which reference could be made. The bishop's teaching must be in accordance with Scripture, whose canon was being defined with gradually increasing precision. But the variety of possible interpretations, as great then as now, made it difficult to settle issues in that way. Similarly appeal could be made to the broad sense of the church's message, reflected in the creeds; but in the kinds of dispute that arose both sides could usually claim with some plausibility to be staying loyal to that broader sense. Or again, church councils could be called to settle the issue. But these often proved open to manipulation in its own interest by one party to the dispute, and were sometimes liable to intimidation by imperial authority.

So the practical necessities of the church's life gave rise to a complex pattern of authorities with the figure of the bishop at its heart. This did not put an end to disputes. There were no clear-cut solutions. It was never possible to provide undisputed answers to the problems that arose. What developed was a set of checks and balances of the sort that any society needs, as it tries to remain true to its original ideals in changing circumstances. But these developing authorities came to be regarded in the church as much more than mere matters of expediency. They were God's provision for the church, and it was important that they should be recognized and respected as such. Claims for their divine authority, especially in the case of the ministry itself, were advanced in increaingly explicit ways. Thus appeals to the local traditions of the great sees, like Rome or Antioch, were made in more and more specific terms. Lists of bishops were compiled which traced the succession right back to the founding apostle, himself understood to have been chosen and appointed by Jesus – even though in most cases a succession of bishops is very unlikely to have had that sort of direct link with the apostles, often not starting until well after their time. In similar fashion the Bishop of Rome came to be endowed with authority over other bishops by applying Jesus' promise of the keys of the kingdom to Peter, as the story is told in Matthew's Gospel, not to bishops in general as had been done earlier, but specifically to the bishops of Rome as Peter's successors in that office.

The fact that the church developed so firm a structure and so authoritative a leadership, understood to have been directly ordained by God, has been a source both of strength and of weakness. It has helped the church to survive in difficult times, and so to provide a place where faith could be lived and passed on. But it has also contributed to the kinds of corruption to which power so often gives rise that we were considering in the last chapter; it has also encouraged an inflexibility that makes the church often reluctant to change in the face of changed circumstances. Throughout the church's history there has been tension between the leaders in positions of power and people deeply affected by some of the very different emphases of the gospel message. Some protests of this kind, like the Franciscan movement, have been contained within the single body of the church; others have led to schism or division, as at the Reformation. Today, in the Roman Catholic Church where this firmness of structure and authoritative leadership are fully present in the papacy of John Paul II, both the strengths and the weaknesses that stem from them are clearly to be seen.

12

The Inner Life of the Church: Worship and Prayer

What is their point? What do they achieve?

In reviewing the public face of the church, we saw how significant but also how ambivalent have been the roles the church has played in the history of European culture and civilisation. Even if, as I have argued, the church's seriously flawed character does not disprove its claim to be the vehicle of divine life and truth, it certainly puts into question the strong form in which such claims are often made.

But there is another, more internal aspect of the church's life to which we need to attend. Its regular life of worship and prayer is often claimed to be not only its inner soul, but its essential *raison d'être*. Here the difficulty that many feel is of a very different character. Is the worship and prayer-life of the church as we encounter it significant enough? Is it commensurate with claims that in it we are giving effective expression to the central truth about the mysterious and complex world in which we live? For many the experience of sharing in the church's worship ('going to church' as we habitually describe it) hardly seems to measure up to so high-flown a description. The problem has nothing to do with different styles or settings of worship. It can apply as much to an elaborate sung mass or a cathedral evensong as to a breaking of bread in a private house or a Quaker gathering in an austere meeting-house. It is a problem about worship as such. What are we doing as we sing our hymns and psalms of praise, and join in the common prayers?

An early Old Testament story speaks of God smelling the sweet savour of Noah's sacrificial offering after the flood and being so pleased with it that he decides never again to cause such devastation to the earth. We smile at the naiveté of the story. But what of the psalms and hymns that we sing to the 'immortal, invisible God only wise'? Are we being any less naive? The prophet Amos denounces those who think that God will be gratified by the sound of their songs and the music of their lutes as much as he does those who think that their sacrificial offerings will give God pleasure. So what is the point of it all?

The practice of worship embodies a profound paradox. True worship must be utterly unself-regarding, offered to God, for God's glory alone. At the same time the point of worship is not to give God pleasure or benefit of some kind; it is we who are the beneficiaries. This is a paradox that has close parallels in other areas of human experience. It is self-forgetful love for the beloved, for the beloved's sake alone, that gives rise to the deepest joy; if it is contaminated with concern for our own self-gratification, that serves only to inhibit what it seeks too directly to attain. And so it is at every level of experience. Music or sport yield their pleasures most fully to those who enjoy them for what they are in themselves and don't see them just as means of acquiring pleasure. So the purpose of worship is to shift our attention away from ourselves and concentrate it on God as the ultimate embodiment of goodness and love. That, as we have seen, can only be done indirectly and obliquely by drawing in imaginative ways on that cluster of images which point us in the direction of the divine mystery and which have been hallowed by long use. And that is what we do in our worship. It does not always or automatically achieve its goal. But in so far as it does, it opens up some sense of the divine presence which gives depth and focus to all our experience of life. Seen in this perspective, the particular forms of Christian worship are mere vehicles of much deeper things shared by the Christian community.

But other aspects of church worship strike a very different note. In petition and intercession we, and our needs, are very much in evidence. We may not often pray for rain or for fine weather, as the church used frequently to do. But we do pray for the sick, for peace in the various strife-torn regions of the world, and for the victims of flood, famine and terrorism. What is it that we are doing? Do we expect our prayers to affect what happens to those for whom we pray? Will God act differently towards them as a result of our prayers, and if so how? Or is the whole process a form of self-delusion?

The origins of such prayers certainly go back to times when the interconnectedness of our ordered world was far less well understood than it is now, and direct intervention of God in the world more widely assumed. Our changing knowledge of the world has led to changes in the content of our petitions and intercessions, such as prayers for rain or fine weather. But that is not enough to solve the problem. I have already argued much earlier that the case against God's providential ordering of the world, on the scale that effective answers to our prayers would involve, is too strong to be denied. So what is the point of such prayers?

The purpose of worship, I have been arguing, is the bringing of our selves and our lives into conscious acknowledgment and awareness of the all-pervading and potentially transforming presence of God. That implies that it must be the real us, not some make-believe idealized version of what we think we ought to be, but ourselves with our actual wants and hopes and fears and loves, that are brought into God's presence. Petition and intercession are forceful ways of ensuring that those rightful concerns, which are an essential part of us, are not forgotten or ignored in the context of worship. The form of the language, which we inherit and continue to employ, can admittedly mislead. But that, as we have seen, is an unavoidable feature of all the language that we have to use in our attempts to relate our lives to the mystery of God. God is not the magician who adjusts the particularities of life at our request, but God is one whose loving presence has the power to transform our experience of every eventuality of life. To abstain from such forms of prayer would be to narrow and impoverish both our worship and our relationship to God.

This approach to the understanding of prayer can perhaps best be illustrated by some reflections on the most representative and traditional of all Christian prayers, namely the Lord's Prayer. It begins with a focussing of attention on God, and the offering of adoration ('hallowed be thy name'). Before it moves on to petitions for our own particular needs, these are first set in the context of God's universal purpose for the world ('thy kingdom come'). Then follow petitions for our physical and personal needs ('give us this day our daily bread'; 'forgive us our trespasses as we forgive those who trespass against us'). The ultimate source whereby all such needs are met is the loving creativity of God, but neither request implies that we have no part to play in meeting them. We are not looking for manna from heaven which by-passes human labour and co-operation, any more than (as the prayer explicitly reminds us) we can look for forgiveness apart from our own readiness to forgive. But the prayer can transform those basic human actions for us by placing them in their proper relation to the all-encompassing purposes of God. So the prayer ends, as it began, with the absolute primacy of God ('thine is the kingdom, the power and the glory, for ever and ever').

13

Morality

*Does Christian faith make any
difference to morality?*

Some readers may feel that much of what I have been writing
about so far is too theoretical, too removed from the practi-
calities of daily life, to constitute what really matters. For
them it is not right belief but right conduct that makes a true
Christian. The teaching of Jesus as they find it in the Sermon
on the Mount is what appeals to them most. Their worry
about Christianity is not so much the truth of its claims about
Jesus, but whether it has a distinctive moral teaching applicable to the complex world in which we find ourselves today,
and whether it makes a difference in practice to how its followers live their lives.

Many religious people are impatient with such an attitude;
Christian faith, they insist, should not be reduced to a matter
of ethics. But the attitude they criticize has a good deal of support in both the Old Testament and the New. 'Is not this the
fast that I have chosen,' says the prophet speaking in the name
of God, 'to loose the fetters of injustice, ... to set free those who
have been crushed, to share your food with the hungry and to
take the homeless poor into your house?' And in the familiar
parable of the sheep and the goats it is those who have minis-
tered to the hungry, the thirsty, the stranger, the naked, the sick
and the prisoners who turn out to have served God in the way
that counts at the day of judgment. How Christianity affects
the way we act is a criterion of judgment that it cannot evade.
And we have already seen enough to recognize that it is a
criterion that provides plenty of ammunition to its foes.

In trying to reflect on the bundle of questions that this issue raises, I want to concentrate on two primary questions: 1. Does Christianity provide us with a moral teaching that is distinct from anything a purely secular morality does or could teach? and 2. Does Christianity provide a stronger motive power for living out its moral teaching than any secular morality is able to offer?

1. In the past Christian moral teaching has often been presented as an absolute obligation to do the will of God, as revealed in Scripture or given through the teaching of God's accredited representatives in the church. But there are strong arguments, of both a theoretical and a practical kind, against that way of determining our moral duty. As we have already seen, neither the Bible nor the leadership of the church can properly claim to be reliable embodiments of God's will with that kind of absolute claim on our obedience. Moreover in practice such authoritative teaching can be seen, too often for comfort, to have served the interests of those in authority. No such authoritarian basis for moral teaching is acceptable. However fallible it may be, the critical judgment of our own moral reasoning has an indispensable part to play. There is nothing revolutionary about that insistence. The history of Christian moral thought has in fact been much less uniformly authoritative in character than the popular version of it that I have been criticizing would suggest. The Catholic tradition in particular has allowed a significant role to the concept of 'natural law', the idea that moral reflection and reasoning, without recourse to the specific revealed teachings of Scripture and the church, can provide Christians with important moral guidance. But today we appear to be faced with an ever-increasing range of moral questions for which neither moral reasoning nor specific religious teaching seems able to provide much help. Take any list of such issues – abortion, birth control, capital punishment, divorce, ecology, feminism, genetic engineering, homosexuality, right through to zero tolerance – and you will find Christians, using specifically Christian arguments, among the more vehement supporters

on both sides of each such disputed question. Christians may claim to have distinctive things to say on such matters, but the things they have to say seem to constitute a set of mutually incompatible convictions.

Does all this mean that there is no such thing as a distinctive Christian moral teaching? If by that is meant: is there a single, authorized Christian moral judgment on each of the important moral questions with which our society is continually being faced, then the answer is clearly 'No'. The nature of the sources from which such judgments are drawn and the nature of the actual judgments that are forthcoming both provide incontrovertible evidence against any such claim. Indeed reflection on the nature of the problems themselves may well lead us to doubt whether they are even in principle susceptible of such decisive resolution. Christianity's inability to provide decisive answers, any more than secular moralists are able to, should not be matter for surprise – indeed what is really worrying is that some Christians claim that it can.

But disavowal of all such claims does not preclude there being a Christian way of approaching moral questions that may be both distinctive and important. Moral judgments are not arrived at simply by a process of detached intellectual argument, however rigorously pursued. They do call for careful reasoning, but first and foremost they are an expression of our values, an outcome of the kind of people that we are. The form that they take depends not only on the clarity of our thinking but more fundamentally on a wide range of our basic beliefs and attitudes concerning the nature of the world and the purpose of human life. Everyone has basic beliefs and attitudes of one sort or another – even if they never give them conscious expression. The Christian's underlying vision of the world is shaped by belief in God and by what I have been calling the Christian story. That story is, as we have seen, open to a variety of interpretations, but it is not infinitely malleable. It does have sufficient overall shape or direction to influence the way a Christian is likely to look at moral issues. It tells a story of God's universal love for the world and for humankind, and of God's sacrificial self-giving on their behalf. And it sees that as the paradigm for human action. This motif underlies the moral teaching of Old and New Testaments alike. The Ten Commandments are not presented in the Old Testament simply as the arbitrary dictates of God; they are described as the appropriate response of Israel to the God who has rescued them from the oppression of Pharaoh ('I am the Lord your God who brought you out of Egypt, out of the land of slavery. You shall have no other God besides me . . .'). So too in the New Testament it is the sacrificial death of Christ on the cross that shapes the high measure of mutual care and forgiveness expected of the early Christian communities ('Live in love as Christ loved you and gave himself up on your behalf'). The shape of Christian morality is determined by its response to the shape of the Christian story in its depiction of the self-giving love of God. The most characteristic feature of that morality is, therefore, to be seen in what is sometimes spoken of as 'a bias to the poor', a sense of responsibility for those in need through whatever cause.

Such an approach does not determine the precise form that any Christian moral judgment will take; it does not carry with it a straightforward application to every human situation. That is something that has still to be worked out in each particular case, in ways that need to call on a wide range of reasoning and experience, much of it from right outside the Christian sphere. If that aspect of the task is forgotten or played down, the consequences can be catastrophic. Good intentions unaccompanied by careful attention to the facts of the case can do much harm. And when Christians do give the careful attention to the detailed implications of each case that is required, they are as likely to make mistakes there as anyone else. But that does nothing to detract from the crucial importance of the particular underlying vision of the good that shapes the overall aims and objectives of Christian moral judgments.

This fundamental character of Christian moral judgment

poses special problems for the public stance of the church on moral issues. Many of the social evils of our time – poverty, homelessness, injustice – are not the direct outcome of individual wrongdoing. They are an inevitable outcome of the political, economic and judicial systems under which people live. But those are things that cannot be changed overnight, and it is often hard to know how they might be changed for the better. Yet the evils are ones with which the church should be seriously concerned. But how? If the church says nothing it will appear to be uncaring, tolerant of injustice. If it does speak, its pronouncements are likely to be heard either as ineffective generalities or as proposals that lack the complex political and economic understanding that is needed. Those are risks that have to be run. Christian involvement is called for at the corporate and at the individual level. Public pronouncements of as informed a nature as can be achieved and the participation of individual Christians in the places where effective decisions are made both have a role to play.

2. Finding answers to the complex moral issues of the day is an important matter. But it is not the most fundamental aspect of morality. Still more basic is the issue raised by the second of the two questions posed at the beginning of this chapter, namely the capacity to live consistently by the moral standards that we do unhesitatingly affirm. The shortcomings in this respect of so much Christian behaviour cannot be denied. But there is no way of measuring how well or how badly the church compares with other moral communities. The best that can be done is to point to some of the resources that Christianity brings to the strengthening of the moral life.

In this regard the role of the Christian story is every bit as significant as it is in determining the content of Christian moral teaching. Christian morality, as I have been describing it, is not so much a matter of obedience to commands as of the imitation of God; not so much a matter of doing what God says, as of doing what God does. This intimate link between our moral duty and our understanding of the nature of God is a powerful motivating force in moral practice. The link is developed in Christian spiritual thought in a number of imaginative ways. The Christian is motivated not only by gratitude and by the desire to imitate the ways of God, powerful though those motives are. One account of the goal of Christian life is growth in the likeness of Christ; on that account the moral life is less a matter even of doing what God does, and more a matter of becoming what God is. Or again the parable of the sheep and the goats, mentioned at the start of this chapter, describes acts of kindness done to those in need as being done to Christ himself ('inasmuch as you did it to one of the least of these, you did it to me'). Seen like that, acts of service present themselves vividly and directly as acts of service to God or to Christ.

The heart of the moral life is not the ability to make agonizing sacrifices against our natural inclinations on the altar of duty; it is rather the training of our desires in love of the good. It is here that Christianity's great potential lies. In the discipline of worship, prayer and meditation our moral ideals are held constantly before us, integrated into the more personal response of love and adoration offered to God. However we understand the working of divine grace, this basic pattern of Christian piety is a powerful way of inculcating the way of virtue at the deepest level of human life.

A final word. If that account sounds a bit too good to be true, recall that it is offered as an account of Christian *resources* or Christian *potential* for strengthening moral practice. And it has its own dangers. By bringing together morality and belief about God in such a close synthesis, the rightness of our beliefs about God becomes crucial. False beliefs about God will produce false beliefs about morality. They have often done so, sometimes disastrously. But true beliefs about God, as we have seen, do not lie in the open, ready to be adopted free from doubt or question. The significance of the Christian story does not lie self-evidently on the surface; it has to be interpreted, and moral criteria are an important part of that process of interpretation. There is an inescapable circularity here – as there is in all moral judgments, since they necessarily derive in part from our overall view of the world which is itself in part determined by our moral sense. So while Christian moral convictions gain strength from their integration into a wider religious view of God, the world and human nature, they still need to remain open to revision, as all our convictions have to do. Perhaps that combination of strong motivation and openness to revision is what is most needed in a world that suffers so much from forms of both moral indifference and moral dogmatism.

14

The Problem of Evil

Does it rule out faith in a good and loving God?

Throughout our discussion the problem of evil has been lurking in the background, threatening to undermine the whole edifice of a reasoned faith that might otherwise be seeming to emerge. How can a world that contains such natural disasters as the floods and earthquakes that sweep away whole communities, such human enormities as Hiroshima and the Holocaust, and such personal tragedies as children born with an incurable, crippling disease or killed by a drunken driver be the creation of an all-powerful and all-loving God, let alone be under such a God's providential care? The problem is too well known to require further description, but is none the less telling for that. Can anything be said in response?

Attempts to answer the question have been given a special name – 'theodicy'. Literally the word means 'the justification of God'. Some people regard it as an improper, even blasphemous undertaking. As the Reformation insisted, it is God who 'justifies' us, not the other way round. The question, it can also be said, is not one that finds much place in Scripture. Job voices his desire to present his complaints before God, but when he finds himself in God's presence he withdraws his challenge. Jesus repudiates the widely held view that the fate of the man born blind or that of the victims of the collapse of the tower of Siloam and of Pilate's tyranny were to be explained by any special sinfulness on the part of the victims. But he offers no other explanation. He turns the question, and sees such tragedies as an opportunity for the exercise of

God's healing grace or as a reminder of the universal need for repentance. The primary Christian response in the face of evil is a practical one: what is to be done in the light of it? All that is true, and it serves to put our original question in a wider perspective; evil is a practical as well as a theoretical problem. But it does nothing whatsoever to disallow the legitimacy of the question or to diminish its force. Faith is not a matter of believing against the evidence. Evidence that seems to call in question the love or the justice of God cannot simply be set aside; it must be squarely faced.

So what can be said? The examples given at the outset can be divided into two main categories: human evils, like the Holocaust and the drunken driver, where human responsibility for the evil is clear; and natural evils, like an earthquake or a genetic malformation, which arise from factors beyond human control. The distinction between the two is real though not absolute. A famine may be due in part to abnormal conditions beyond human control, but its inception may have been due also to greedy exploitation of the soil in the past and its effects accentuated by greedy exploitation of shortages in the present. The growth of scientific knowledge on topics such as global warming and genetics are all the time extending the range where human responsibility operates. But though the dividing line between them may be continually shifting and there may always be a grey area, there is, for anyone who is not prepared to deny the concepts of human freedom and human responsibility altogether, a significant difference between the two categories of 'human' and 'natural' evils.

But to acknowledge that distinction does not let God off the hook, even in the case of human evils. It is still the case that God is the creator, and has created human beings with a capacity for horrendous evil. But we were not created fresh-minted, straight from the hand of God. The human race has emerged through a long and gradual process of evolution, and each individual recapitulates something of that development as he or she grows from infancy to maturity. Perhaps that is the only kind of way in which human persons with a capacity for love, freely offered and received, could be brought into existence. And perhaps that emergence of freedom necessarily involves the capacity for wrong and evil choices. It is sometimes suggested that God could have created human beings with genuine freedom, who nonetheless invariably chose the good. But I doubt whether such an idea is coherent. If we try to imagine a world in which all evil is thought away while everything else is left as it is, the vision soon begins to dissolve. The 'we' of such an imaginary world would be so different from the actual 'we' that it is questionable whether we are really able to envisage it; the people inhabiting it would be a different species from ourselves. So perhaps human evil in some form is an unavoidable aspect of any world that could give rise to a society of human persons ruled by freely given love towards God and one another. It may well be so, though it cannot be more than a matter of speculation. But even if it is, it does not go far to remove our sense of problem. The sheer volume of evil and misery that the history of human life reveals seems out of all proportion. If that was the risk God took, has not the risk gone badly wrong?

Natural evils are not open even to that line of reflection. The Genesis myth admittedly hints that they might be. In the story the sin of Adam and Eve has repercussions not only on future human behaviour, but also on the processes of nature ('In pain you will bring forth children . . . and only by the sweat of your brow will you win your bread'). But for us who know human life to be a late emergent on our planet, there can be no such direct link between the disorder of human behaviour and the disorder of the natural world. Yet there is a clear link between the natural and the human worlds. The physical conditions that characterize our planet have made possible the emergence of human life, while other parts of our universe preclude it. More broadly, human life as we know it requires a stable background with the kind of regularities that the physical world displays. Without a constancy of physical properties in the world that we inhabit there could be no social interaction, no planning for action in the future. But that same constancy, so vital to any form of ordered living, gives rise also to damage and disaster; its inexorable ways do not change in face of human need. The fire that burns to keep us warm is the same fire that destroys by burning; the water that gives life to our crops by falling as rain is the same water that destroys them by flooding. Perhaps something like the conditions in which human life has developed, with their mixture of blessing and curse, is necessary to the emergence and sustaining of human life. Such reflections are even more speculative than those about the implications of human freedom. At most they are reminders that evil is not a feature that could simply be excised from our world, leaving everything else essentially the same. It is too deeply embedded in the structure of things. A world free of it would be a wholly different sort of world. But the fundamental difficulty is still there. The sheer volume of evil and the horrendous nature of its consequences stand in sharp conflict with faith in a loving, creator God.

So the problem remains. Whatever the value of the the lines of argument I have proposed, they most emphatically do not 'solve' the problem. The extent and the enormity of evil do constitute evidence against belief in a loving God. What my suggestions may claim to do is to show that the case is more complex than it appears at first sight. The problem of evil is a damaging blow piercing the theist's armour, but it is not the clear-cut, knock-out blow it is often taken to be. There is still scope for other considerations to be entered.

If we allow the problem of evil to destroy belief in God altogether, we get rid of one intractable problem only to be faced with another. For we are then faced with the 'problems' of existence and of goodness. The theist has to admit that evil is a dark mystery. But those who reject belief in God are faced with a corresponding mystery. How is it that there is anything at all? How is it that the random interaction of physical matter should by itself have given rise not only to human life, but also to the qualities of love and goodness by which it is characterized as surely as it is characterized by terrible evil? The dark mystery of evil is replaced by the dazzling mystery of good.

If we do not allow the problem of evil to destroy belief in God altogether, are we then bound to adopt the stance of Ivan Karamazov who denounced as wholly unacceptable the creation of any world, however great the happiness to which it might give rise, if it involved the unavenged tears of one innocent child? The moral challenge of such a stance is extremely strong. It should certainly hold us back from ever saying that we can offer a 'final solution' of the problem. But even among those whose lives have been marked by the most intense suffering, there are surprisingly few Ivan Karamazovs who would rather that the world, and they themselves, had never existed. Here too the issue, grave though its threat to theistic faith most certainly is, is not quite as clear cut as it at first appears.

So far I have been discussing the problem of evil as a challenge to faith in God in general terms. I have been assuming that the God with whom we are concerned in the discussion is all-loving and all-powerful, and that takes us some way towards focussing the discussion specifically on the God of Christian faith. But not all the way. The Christian story, as we have recalled throughout this book, presents the creative power and the redemptive love of God in its own particular way through the biblical narrative. At the heart of that record is the crucifixion of Christ, seen as the saving revelation of God. Does this central tenet of Christian faith help to illuminate the dark mystery of evil?

We drew a distinction at the start of this discussion between human evils, where human responsibility is involved, and natural evils, where it is not. It is primarily with the former that the significance of the crucifixion has traditionally been linked. 'Christ died for our sins.' 'He died that we might be forgiven.' What the crucifixion offers is not an explanation of why human evil exists, but the promise of God's provision for coping with it. But to many even that provision appears suspect; in their eyes it begins by unhealthily emphasizing the emotion of guilt and then undertakes to deal with it by the morally questionable claim that Christ underwent the punishment of death that should have been inflicted on us. Those criticisms are true of some forms of Christian imagery and preaching, but the meaning of the cross can be expressed in very different terms that are not open to those particular objections.

To deny the reality of guilt altogether is, as I have already argued, to deny human responsibility and thereby to deny an essential element of what it is to be human. We have only to consider the recent history of South Africa, of Northern Ireland and of Bosnia, to recognize the entail of bitterness and guilt left by past crimes, and the difficulty of breaking it. It cannot be simply ignored or forgotten, but it has to be broken, or it will continue to wreak havoc in the future. In essence the crucifixion is a story of what human wickedness can do and of how the way of love can remain unbroken by it. Only in such a context, where the evilness of evil is not denied but its consequences are accepted without giving rise to yet further evil by way of retaliation, can the forgiveness that is so desperately needed be morally given and received, and men and women set free for the creation of a different future. But the story of the cross is not simply the story of a heroic past event. For the Christian it is also to be seen as the saving revelation of God; it is a powerful symbolic story embodying God's way of response to human sin and evil. It depicts the power of God as the power of persuasive love rather than the power of coercive force, and the love of God as unlimited both in its scope and in its commitment. As such it expresses not only God's way of forgiveness and redemption, but the response of God to natural evil also. For the cross depicts God's self-identification with human suffering. In the belief that God stands not only over and above them but alongside them in their struggle, many have found reinforcement in their own fight against evil and help in their own endurance of suffering. But whatever the practical help that conviction may provide, it does not, we must repeat, 'solve' the problem. What it does do is to show that, if we start from the world as it is with all its attendant evil and suffering, then God as depicted by Christian faith stands in the only morally conceivable relation to it. But there is still a place, within the life of faith, for the anguished protest of Job. Indeed it is even there in the story of the cross itself. In the account of Mark, the earliest Gospel, the one word that Jesus speaks from the cross is a word of protest: 'My God, my God, why hast thou forsaken me?' God's self-identification is not only with our fight against evil and with our suffering, but also with our protest against the dark mystery of evil itself.

Earlier on I insisted that for the Christian story the crucifixion is not to be thought of as an event on its own, but that cross-and-resurrection need to be seen as two parts of a single whole. So far in this discussion I have been disobeying that injunction. That needs to be put right, for the resurrection is highly pertinent to it. But there are serious problems to be faced in doing so; to these we must now turn.

15

Death

Is that the end?

A hope for life beyond death was something that was beginning to gain ground at the start of the Christian era. In the Greek world the mystery religions exercised a strong appeal; and in the Jewish world a newly emerging hope of resurrection had helped to sustain the martyrs of Jewish resistance in the second century BC and was a part of the teaching of the Pharisees of Jesus' day. It was also at the heart of the Christian message from the outset. Paul's address to the Council of the Areopagus at Athens, for example, is summed up as being 'about Jesus and the resurrection'. For many of that sophisticated Gentile audience, talk of resurrection was sufficient reason to dismiss Paul's preaching out of hand; but at a more popular level it proved an important part of Christianity's appeal. It took a variety of forms. Sometimes it drew, as Jews also did, on Greek ideas of the immortality of the soul, but more characteristically it took the form of the resurrection of the body, the form in which it is enshrined in the creed. At first what was looked for seems to have been a general resurrection, when all the dead would be raised as part of an expected return of Christ and an end to human history. As that particular expectation faded, the hope became focussed more on the individual's survival of death. But throughout most of Christian history the underlying conviction remained that this world, even though the good creation of God, was first and foremost a preparation for life with God in another eternal world. And that conviction provided a perspective which influenced every aspect of Christian teaching and piety in the centuries that followed.

But is that hope one that can reasonably be held in any form today? Modern studies of the genes and of the brain have greatly extended our recognition of the close inter-relation between the physical and the non-physical aspects of human life. That doesn't mean that their relation is no longer problematic for us; the nature of the relationship remains as mysterious as ever. But even so, the increasing recognition of how closely they are bound up with one another poses acute difficulties for the idea of human survival of death. In the first place it makes the idea of a non-physical soul as the essential person, which is able to survive bodily death and enjoy immortality free from the restraints of the body, very difficult to entertain. The body is integral to the only kind of personal being that we know. So the resurrection of the body, which has often been seen in the past as a primitive and outmoded form of the Christian hope, begins to re-emerge as the most intelligible form of it. But that does nothing to remove the obvious difficulties inherent in the concept of bodily resurrection, difficulties of a kind that critics of Christianity have brought against it from the earliest days – taunts, for example, about what would happen in a case of cannibalism with two people laying claim to elements of the same physical body! And it doesn't need to take the form of jibes like that. Quite simply we know what happens to the physical body after death. A bodily future of some kind may be the most intelligible way of conceiving a person's survival of death; but is it a credible one?

The issue is important on two scores. In the first place the universality of death poses precisely the kind of ultimate question about the meaning and purpose of life which is at the heart of every religious faith. It is something which every religion needs to address. But it is also of particular importance in the context of the kind of answer that I have just been offering to the intractable problem of evil. If suffering and evil are in some way necessary concomitants of the freedom required for the development of human persons, then, if there is no survival of death, we have to acknowledge that in a vast number of cases that development is cut short long before it has had time to bear any fruit at all.

How can we respond to difficulties of such magnitude? The most obvious place for a Christian to begin is with the resurrection of Jesus. For it is Jesus' resurrection that is traditionally emphasized as the ground of hope for the Christian's own resurrection. But the issue cannot be settled as easily as that. As we have already had occasion to see, we are not in a position to know just what happened to give rise to the records of Jesus' resurrection. The Gospels are not the kind of documents to provide an answer to that question. So we cannot point to the resurrection of Jesus as if it constituted incontrovertible proof that one man has died and returned to life and that therefore the possibility of life beyond death is assured. But that is not to say that the resurrection of Jesus is irrelevant to our search. In that earlier discussion I described it as a symbolic truth, affirming that death does not have the last word about human life. However, it has that significance, not as an isolated event on its own, but as a climactic moment in the wider Christian story of God's dealings with the world. The precise implications of the story of the resurrection will depend on how we read that wider story. I have been presenting it as the story of God's creative and redemptive purpose to bring into being a world of men and women living in relations of love towards one another and towards God. New Testament writers speak of the life of the newly emerging church as a first stage in the fulfilment of that purpose. 'Risen life in Christ' and 'eternal life' are used there not just as phrases to describe how life will be after death; they are ways of speaking about Christian life here and now. Humans have been taken into a relationship with God of such intensity that it is inconceivable to envisage it ever being broken. 'Eternal life' is a qualitative as well as a temporal description.

That way of putting the matter shifts the emphasis in relation to death away from a single event to the broader concept of the character of God. Such a shift is consistent with the response of Jesus to the Sadducees in the Gospel record. Dealing with one of those crude but telling objections to the idea of bodily resurrection – in this case, whose wife would a woman who has remarried seven times after the death of her husband be when all have been resurrected – Jesus affirms the reality of life beyond death by insisting that 'God is not God of the dead but of the living'. In other words, the relationship of intimacy and love between God and human beings, which is God's purpose for the world and which is in part being realized already in Christian life, is of such a nature that the idea of its extinction by the fact of physical death is simply unthinkable; it would contradict the whole fabric of belief in God. It is this conviction, much more broadly based than on a single event in the past, that the final word rests with God rather than with death that finds such powerful symbolic expression in the resurrection of Jesus.

My emphasis in the discussion so far has been on how closely the question of the finality of death is tied up with the whole structure and logic of Christian belief in God. But we still have to face the question: does our contemporary understanding of what it is to be a human being simply rule out the whole notion of the survival of death as inconceivable? We need to ask whether there is any response to the claim that neither the immortality of the soul nor the resurrection of the body provides a credible model for conceiving life beyond death.

We must begin by reiterating a point already made. When we acknowledge that a human being is a 'psycho-somatic unity', a complex organism in which the physical and the non-physical are inextricably intertwined, we are not claiming that we have come to a full understanding of what it is to be a human person. Rather we are eliminating certain ways of thinking about human beings as made up of two separable entities, such as a non-physical soul contained within a physical body. But the relation of the physical and the non-physical aspects of our being remains a mystery; we simply do not know how to conceive it. The more we recognise the powerful influence of our origins, genetic and environmental, the more puzzling become our apparent freedom and our sense of responsibility for what we make or fail to make of that inheritance. To deny that we have any such freedom or responsibility is to go against a fundamental aspect of our experience and to deny what is most distinctively human about us. We can't get away from the puzzling question of how it is that we are able to contribute to shaping what is apparently given to us in our origins. How is it that we can, as we put it, 'make something of ourselves'? Reflection on questions such as these is likely to lead to the conclusion that, inescapable as they are, such questions are incapable of being answered. We can analyse particular aspects of how a human being functions, but there is no external standing ground from which we can observe and assess how human beings function in their totality. We can study the brain and the mind and observe how intimately they depend on one another. But the we who do the observing and assess its results escape the observer's net. The whole is greater than its parts, and we indicate our recognition of that fact by the use of other words, such as person, self or spirit. In short, what it is to be a human person necessarily transcends our capacity to understand. It is ultimately and impenetratably mysterious to us.

There is an analogy here with belief in God. In the opening chapter of the book I spoke of belief in God as a way of responding to the mystery of how it is that there is anything at all, and stressed that any language we use of God must necessarily be of a metaphorical or symbolic nature. There are grounds for believing in God, but the very nature of the belief itself implies that how the language we are led to use is properly to be understood in its application to God is something that will always lie beyond our grasp. So in a similar way it is the fundamentally mysterious nature of the human person that justifies our expressing hopes of a human destiny beyond death, even when we are unable to conceive how such hopes might be fulfilled. How could we expect to be able to form a conception of it, when the nature of human persons is necessarily mysterious and not just an area of knowledge that we have not yet mastered?

How far do such reflections help us? They are, I think, a proper counter to any claim that all hope of life beyond death can be shown to be an utter impossibility. And that is precisely what we needed to show in the context of the argument of this chapter. For it makes it reasonable for us to hold on to the hope that we have seen to be so integral to the Christian story. But that is as far as they take us. Talk about an immortal soul or a resurrected body is as symbolic as talk about the music of heaven or the flames of hell, the second coming of Christ and the final day of judgment. These are not beliefs that enable us to predict or to picture what will happen at some future date. They are ways of expressing a faith that the final word lies with God rather than with death, and that that final word involves God's human creation. Beyond that neither our knowledge or our imagination can reach.

Epilogue

It is time to take stock. Where does this process of reasoned reflection on some fundamental questions about Christian faith leave us?

One thing is clear: the questions and difficulties have not been resolved and got out of the way. The answers, of course, are my own and other Christians would have answered many of them differently. But even if the discussion had been developed at greater length and the arguments conducted with greater skill than this book has achieved, the outcome on this score would have been the same. Many of the questions we have been pursuing are simply not of a kind that are accessible to definitive resolution. So the questions remain with us.

That should not be a matter for surprise. Whatever our overall interpretation of life, be it humanist, materialist or what you will, and however carefully we may have thought it through, there will always turn out to be aspects of our experience and of the world that don't seem to fit. Part of what I hope to have shown is that in that respect Christian faith is in no different position from any other way of interpreting and living in the world. We are all faced with residual questions and difficulties that we are unable to sort out. So what matters most about the reflections I have offered is not so much whether they convince the reader but whether they provide a useful stimulus and model for continued wrestling with those questions in the future. For the questions are ones that, at one level or another, impinge on every thoughtful Christian. We cannot help but be aware of them. To pretend they don't exist is to introduce an element of 'bad faith' into our Christianity. We need to find our own ways of engaging with them from within the context of our Christian faith.

Looking back on this series of questions and the reflections to which they have given rise, two things stand out for me. First, although many of the questions are as old as Christian faith itself, the particular form in which they impose themselves on us today often derives from recent knowledge; the way we experience them is influenced by what the latest discoveries of history or science have taught us. We are right to take that knowledge seriously and to ask what impact it has on our Christian faith. But sometimes we are too confident about our new knowledge. We treat it as if it were the complete and unchanging truth of things. We forget that much of it is the outcome of some one restricted area of research, and that even in that setting it will no doubt yield place in due course to further new research. The second thing concerns the faith rather than the questions. That too we tend to think of as more complete and more unchanging than it really is. There is a continuity between the faith as it was professed by the earliest Christians or in the Middle Ages and the faith as it is held today. But there are great differences in belief too. The way Christians believe has changed substantially through the ages, and will continue to change.

So bringing reason to bear on faith in the light of modern knowledge does not involve a clash between two fixed and unchanging approaches to the world; it is not the meeting of an irresistible force with an immovable object. Neither the new insights from modern discoveries nor Christian faith can lay claim to secure and certain knowledge. Both are engaged in voyages of discovery that involve the recognition of limitations in past views that were once thought to be true beyond question. The conflicts between the two, real and serious though they often are, do not always prove to be as direct as they appear at first sight. For the believer the pursuit of such reasoned reflection is a necessary part of the way in which faith establishes its credentials in each generation and learns how to express itself in a rapidly changing world.

Reason and faith are not polar opposites. Reason is integral to the life of faith; it helps to distinguish it from mere prejudice or superstition. The faith by which a Christian lives is fully compatible with a continuing search to understand better what the content of that faith should be.

Biblical texts cited or referred to

Further Reading

The book lists that follow have been compiled with a particular purpose in view. They are designed for people with little or no background knowledge of theology who have read this book and want to pursue in more detail some of the lines of thought that are briefly outlined here. They are a personal selection of books which by and large follow the same kind of approach to the subject that I have done. The books in each section are arranged roughly in an order of increasing complexity, starting with the more straightforward and introductory and ending with the more detailed and advanced.

General

Keith Ward, *The Living God*, SPCK 1984
John Hick, *The Second Christianity*, SCM Press 1983
Hans Küng, *Credo*, SCM Press 1993
J.L.Houlden, *Connections*, SCM Press 1986
Maurice Wiles, *Faith and the Mystery of God*, SCM Press 1982
    Four of these books are outline expositions of central Christian beliefs by scholars writing for a general readership. *Connections* is the odd one out; it offers interesting reflections on what is involved in attempting such a task.

1. Beginnings

Martin Prozesky, *A New Guide to the Debate about God*, SCM Press 1992
Austin Farrer, *A Science of God?*, Geoffrey Bles 1966
John Polkinghorne, *Science and Creation*, SPCK 1988
Keith Ward, *God, Chance and Necessity*, One World 1996
Ian Barbour, *Religion and Science*, SCM Press 1998

Prozesky sets out in a balanced way the cases for and against belief in God. Farrer's approach is more philosophical, but with that imaginative touch that characterized so much of his writing. The last three books deal specifically with the issue of religion and science. Ward concentrates on the mechanical or determinist implications of science that seem to some to rule out belief in God, while Barbour's book is much the biggest and most comprehensive of the three.

Interlude I: Language

G.B.Caird, *The Language and Imagery of the Bible*, Duckworth 1980
John Macquarrie, *God-Talk*, SCM Press 1967
Ian Barbour, *Myths, Models and Paradigms*, SCM Press 1974
Janet Martin Soskice, *Metaphor and Religious Language*, OUP 1985
These are all fairly demanding treatments of a difficult topic. Caird's book, as its title shows, has a more restricted aim than the other three. Soskice's book is particularly concerned to show how metaphorical language can function as a means of conveying how things are and not just how we feel.

2. The God of the Bible

T.J.Gorringe, *God's Theatre*, SCM Press 1991
Maurice Wiles, *God's Action in the World*, SCM Press 1986
Both books discuss the problems involved in the idea of God's providential control of the world.

Interlude II: Using the Bible

Etienne Charpentier, *How to Read the Old Testament*, SCM Press 1982
Etienne Charpentier, *How to Read the New Testament*, SCM Press 1982
John Barton, *Making the Christian Bible*, Darton, Longman and Todd 1997
John Barton, *People of the Book? The Authority of the Bible in Christianity*, SPCK 1993
J.L.Houlden, *Bible and Belief*, SPCK 1991

Harry.Y.Gamble, *The New Testament Canon: Its Making and Meaning*, Fortress Press 1985
Dennis Nineham, *The Use and Abuse of the Bible*, Macmillan 1976
The first two books are very informative practical guides with charts and diagrams rather than books to be read straight through. Barton's *Making the Christian Bible* and Gamble's book both deal with the formation of the canon. The other three are interesting discussions, at differing levels of complexity, of the problems involved in using the Bible as a basis for belief.

3. Son of God

J.L.Houlden, *Jesus: A Question of Identity*, SPCK 1992
John Bowden, *Jesus: The Unanswered Questions*, SCM Press 1988
John Ziesler, *The Jesus Question*, Lutterworth Press 1980
Jaroslav Pelikan, *Jesus through the Centuries*, Yale University Press 1985
John Hick, *The Metaphor of God Incarnate*, SCM Press 1993
Ruth Page, *The Incarnation of Freedom and Love*, SCM Press 1991
The first three books are clear and challenging surveys of the difficulties arising out of modern study and knowledge for determining how we are to understand the figure of Jesus. Pelikan draws on artistic as well as literary evidence to give a fascinating account of the varied ways in which Jesus has been understood down the ages. Hick and Page offer their own contemporary interpretations.

Interlude III: Creeds

Frances Young, *The Making of the Creeds*, SCM Press 1991
C.S.Rodd (ed.), *Foundation Documents of the Faith*, T. & T. Clark 1987
Young's book is an excellent historical account. Rodd's book is a collection of essays by various writers on the principal creeds and the most important confessional statements by the churches down the ages.

4. Birth, Death and Resurrection

H.J.Richards, *The First Christmas: What Really Happened?*, Mowbray 1973
Frances Young, *Sacrifice and the Death of Christ*, SPCK 1975
John Knox, *The Death of Christ*, Collins 1967
G.W.H.Lampe and D.M.MacKinnon, *The Resurrection: A Dialogue*, Mowbray 1966
Paul Avis (ed.), *The Resurrection of Jesus Christ*, SPCK 1975
Stephen Barton and Graham Stanton (ed.), *Resurrection*, SPCK 1994

Richards's book (like the other two of his that figure later in these lists) is written with unusual simplicity and directness. Young and Knox both combine a historical approach with reflection on the meanings given to Christ's death. The three books on the resurrection are all by more than one author. The first is a discussion between two scholars arising out of a broadcast Easter sermon. The essays in Avis's book are of a broad expository kind, whereas the other book is made up of many more shorter pieces dealing with a variety of different aspects of the question.

Interlude IV: Miracles

H.J.Richards, *The Miracles of Jesus: What Really Happened?*, Mowbray 1983
R.H.Fuller, *Interpreting the Miracles*, SCM Press 1963
C.F.D.Moule (ed.), *Miracles*, Mowbray 1965
Ernst and Marie-Luise Keller, *Miracles in Dispute*, SCM Press 1969

These books are very varied in character. Fuller's book is concerned with the miracle stories in the Gospels. Moule's contains a collection of essays – philosophical, biblical and ancient historical. The Kellers' book is a detailed account of the debate about miracle over the last two hundred years.

5. The Christian Story

John Macquarrie, *The Humility of God*, SCM Press 1978
Gerd Theissen, *Biblical Faith*, SCM Press 1984

The first of these books is briefer and more devotional in tone;

the other wrestles with how the story is to be understood in an evolutionary world.

Interlude V: Symbolism

F.W.Dillistone, *The Power of Symbols*, SCM Press 1986
G.Cope, *Symbolism in the Bible and the Church*, SCM Press 1959
The first book is a general discussion of the importance of symbols in human life; the other looks at the role of particular symbols in the Bible and in the history of Christianity.

6. Jesus

Gerd Theissen, *The Shadow of the Galilean*, SCM Press 1987
E.P.Sanders, *The Historical Figure of Jesus*, Penguin Books 1993
A.E.Harvey, *Jesus and the Constraints of History*, Duckworth 1982
The Shadow of the Galilean is in the form of a novel; it is written by a leading New Testament scholar, and is remarkably successful in conveying the context of Jesus' life and ministry. The first three books listed under Chapter 3 all begin with assessments of what can and cannot be known about Jesus. Sanders and Harvey's books are more detailed accounts of the historical evidence and how it should be used.

Interlude VI: Modern Study of the Gospels

R.A.Burridge, *Four Gospels, One Jesus?*, SPCK 1994
C. Tuckett, *Reading the New Testament: Methods and Interpretations*, SPCK 1987
G.N.Stanton, *The Gospels and Jesus*, OUP 1989
Burridge's attractive book begins with a short account of the nature of the Gospels and modern study of them and then looks at the distinct portraits of Jesus in each of them. Tuckett's book is a thorough survey of the different forms and methods of critical study applied to the Gospels, while Stanton shows those methods at work on each of the four Gospels.

7. Spirit

T.J.Gorringe, *Discerning Spirit*, SCM Press 1990
John V.Taylor, *The Go-Between God*, SCM Press 1972
Peter Donovan, *Interpreting Religious Experience*, Sheldon Press
1979
  The first two books both look in a broad and imaginative way
at how God's spirit can be understood to be at work in all
dimensions of human life. Donovan's book is a clear and careful
account of what constitutes religious experience and how it can
best be understood.

8. The Trinity

R.P.C.Hanson, *God: Creator, Saviour, Spirit*, SCM Press 1960
Cyril Richardson, *The Doctrine of the Trinity*, Abingdon Press
1958
G.W.H.Lampe, *God as Spirit*, OUP 1977
  Hanson's book is a relatively straightforward and standard
presentation of the doctrine. The other two books are more
demanding, each developing its own approach to the issue.

Interlude VII: The Development of Doctrine

R.P.C.Hanson, *The Continuity of Christian Doctrine*, Seabury
Press
1981
Robert Wilken, *The Myth of Christian Beginnings*, SCM Press
1979
Maurice Wiles, *The Making of Christian Doctrine*, CUP 1967
Maurice Wiles, *The Remaking of Christian Doctrine*, SCM Press
1974
  Hanson's book again offers a thoughtful presentation of a
relatively standard view. The other three put more stress on the
degree of change within that continuity. Wilken draws examples
from a variety of historical periods. The first of my two books
deals only with the early church, the other with the present time.

9. Salvation

Peter Selby, *Rescue, Jesus and Salvation To-Day*, SPCK 1997
J.A.T.Robinson, *In the End, God. . .*, James Clarke 1950

Vernon White, *Atonement and Incarnation*, CUP 1991
Paul Fiddes, *Past Event and Present Salvation*, Darton, Longman and Todd 1989
  Selby's book approaches the subject from the angle of present need. Robinson tackles the question whether Christian salvation will ultimately include everyone. White and Fiddes wrestle with the problem of how the death of Jesus is a source of salvation in the present.

10. Other Faiths

Maurice Wiles, *Christian Theology and Inter-Religious Dialogue*, SCM Press 1992
Alan Race, *Christians and Religious Pluralism*, SCM Press 1983
  My own book develops the argument of the chapter in this book at more length. Race's book takes a similar view, but gives a good exposition of other attitudes to the question.

11. The Public Face of the Church

Victor de Waal, *What is the Church?*, SCM Press 1969
J.L.Houlden, *The Public Face of the Gospel*, SCM Press 1997
Robert Adolfs, *The Grave of God*, Burns and Oates 1967
R.P.C.Hanson, *The Identity of the Church*, SCM 1987
  De Waal and Hanson's books are broad surveys with differing degrees of detail. Houlden's book looks at the evidence of the New Testament. Adolfs is a Dutch Roman Catholic writer, worried by the present condition of the church and wrestling with the question of how it needs to change if it is to be true to the way of Christ.

Interlude VIII: From Jesus to the Church

W.H.C.Frend, *The Early Church*, SCM Press 1991
Henry Chadwick, *The Early Church*, Penguin 1967
Ian Hazlitt (ed.), *Early Christianity*, SPCK 1991
  The first two books are histories of the early church written by experts for the general reader. Hazlitt's is similar in aim, but takes the form of a series of short essays by different scholars, each dealing with a particular topic.

12: The Inner Life of the Church: Worship and Prayer

T.G.A. Baker,*Questioning Worship*, SCM Press 1977
Peter Baelz, *Does God Answer Prayer?*, Darton, Longman and Todd 1982
Vincent Brümmer, *What Are We Doing When We Pray?*, SCM Press 1984
Peter Baelz, *Prayer and Providence*, SCM Press 1968
Evelyn Underhill, *Worship*, James Nisbet 1936; revised edition Eagle 1991

The titles explain themselves, the first and the last books dealing with the issues discussed in the first half of the chapter, the other three with those in the second half. In both groups there is a considerable difference in the level of treatment between the earlier and later books in the list.

13. Morality

E.F.Carpenter, *Common Sense about Christian Ethics*, Victor Gollancz 1963
Brian Hebblethwaite, *The Adequacy of Christian Ethics*, Marshall, Morgan and Scott 1981
Peter Baelz, *Ethics and Belief*, Sheldon Press 1977
Helen Oppenheimer, *The Character of Christian Morality*, Faith Press 1965
G.R.Dunstan, *The Artifice of Ethics*, SCM Press 1974

All these books are primarily concerned with the distinctive nature of Christian ethics rather than with detailed consideration of particular ethical issues. The differences between them in level of treatment is not particularly great.

14. The Problem of Evil

Melvyn Thompson, *Cancer and the God of Love*, SCM Press 1976
John Cowburn, *Shadows and the Dark*, SCM Press 1979
Brian Hebblethwaite, *Evil, Suffering and Religion*, Sheldon Press 1976
Austin Farrer, *Love Almighty and Ills Unlimited*, Collins 1962
John Hick, *Evil and the God of Love*, Macmillan 1966

The first two are quite short books that bring a practical and imaginative approach to the question. The other three tackle the problems in a more systematic way. Hick's book is much the biggest, including a substantial historical as well as philosophical discussion.

15. Death

H.J.Richards, *Death and After: What Will Really Happen?*, Collins 1980
John Macquarrie, *Christian Hope*, Mowbray 1978
Russell Aldwinckle, *Death in the Secular City*, George Allen and Unwin 1972

Three very different books. Richards's book is brief, with his characteristic virtues of clarity and directness. Macquarrie comes at the issues by way of positive reflection on traditional Christian teaching, while Aldwinckle's book is a good review of the many philosophical difficulties to be faced.